MY ONLY SON: HIS ONLY MOTHER!

Witnessing the Hand of God Through
10 of the Darkest Years

Christopher Watkins & Lugenia Johnson

authorHOUSE®

AuthorHouse™
1663 Liberty Drive
Bloomington, IN 47403
www.authorhouse.com
Phone: 1 (800) 839-8640

Published by AuthorHouse   05/16/2016

ISBN: 978-1-5049-7937-5 (sc)
ISBN: 978-1-5049-7936-8 (e)

Library of Congress Control Number: 2016902378

Print information available on the last page.

Any people depicted in stock imagery provided by Thinkstock are models, and such images are being used for illustrative purposes only. Certain stock imagery © Thinkstock.

This book is printed on acid-free paper.

Because of the dynamic nature of the Internet, any web addresses or links contained in this book may have changed since publication and may no longer be valid. The views expressed in this work are solely those of the author and do not necessarily reflect the views of the publisher, and the publisher hereby disclaims any responsibility for them.

KJV
Scripture quotations marked KJV are from the Holy Bible, King James Version (Authorized Version). First published in 1611. Quoted from the KJV Classic Reference Bible, Copyright © 1983 by The Zondervan Corporation.

DEDICATION

This book is dedicated to the countless men (and women) who, each day, continue to endure the often harsh, uncaring, and somtimes inhumane and dehumanizing treatment of a system that tears down rather than builds up, destroys rather than rehabilitates - a system we refer to as INCARCERATION.

This book is also dedicated to the mothers (fathers) and the innumerable family members and other loved ones who stand by, helpess to rescue their incarcerated loved ones, or, fight against a system that wrongfully slams the iron bars in an individul's face, disciminatedly based on rules that change as the game is played; and, as the players change.

And last, but certainly not least, this book is dedicated to
Mrs. Annie W. Johnson,
my mother and Christopher's Grandmother. She was the greatest inspiration, so loving and kind. She cherished her children, grandchildren, and great-grandchildren with all of her heart, and with her very life. We are saddened by the fact that she did not live to see Christopher recalim his life, his freedom.

Granny, He's Home! We Love & Miss You!

†

FOREWORD

As a single mother with two children whom God had blessed me to love and care for through the joys, challenges, and difficulties of growing up; I never imagined myself in this ten–year ordeal. So many times I asked God "Why? Why, God? Why *MY* son?" So many days I spent driving the countless miles up and down the highways, and sometimes country roads, going to make sure that my son knew that I loved him and was determined to encourage him through this situation. So many times I felt the creepy chill down my spine as I heard the iron doors close behind me each time I entered the buildings that sat in the middle of the barbed wire fences.

God never specifically answered my 'Why?' questions. But what God did was continue to give me revelations, inspirations, and wisdom concerning each situation. What God did was to develop my son's character and cause him to reflect over his life and gain a renewed respect and appreciation for all that his little family unit had endured. God also strengthened my resolve and determination to stand against anything the advesary could send my way. God re-tooled my ministry tool box and gave me sermons that caused countless others to come and surrender their lives to Him while yet others found strength and comfort as they navigated the stormy seas of their daily circumstances.

God did so much more for us, in us and through us than I believe that Chris and I may ever know. And if anyone else will allow Him, God will do the same amd even more for them.

God gave us eveidence, through countless testimonies over these ten years, that He *IS* ALIVE. We serve a *LIVING LORD*! It is our prayer that the words found on the pages of this book will bless you as we have been blessed in the living of these days regardless of how difficult they may have been. Now we know without a shadow of a doubt that "...all things work together to good for those who love the Lord and are the called according to His purpose." (Romans 8:28)

†

TABLE OF CONTENTS

PART ONE

MY ONLY SON

MY ONLY SON

"...and there was darkness over all the earth...and Jesus cried out 'Father, into thy hands I commend my Spirit.'" Luke 23:44 – 46 (AKJV)

Only the man on the center cross seemed to have any family members or friends around him as he suffered on that wooden cross.

As I was preparing to translate into writing my deepest thoughts concerning the evens that my son had endured over the ten years of his incarceration, I realized that Easter, as the world labels it, was not many days away. I prefer to say *'Resurrection Sunday'* rather than *Easter* because of what the day and the entire weekend means to me. And, I truly believe that it should mean as much to the entire Christian community. With that thought, I sat back in my chair, pulled my hands away from the computer keyboard, as a very solemn scene began to flood my thoughts. I could only imagine what Mary, the mother of Jesus, must have experienced in the first century, over 2,000 years ago. As this scene developed in my mind, I believe there must have been a horrible stench of death in the air that day on that hill called Calvary. Hundreds had probably met their deaths, right there, on that same hill because crucifixion was a common manner of Roman execution of criminals in that era.

My mind began to focus on one area of this death scene on Calvary Hill. I imagined that I could see the three crosses, their tops piercing the sky, with a man in excruciating agony hanging from each one. Only the man on the center cross seemed to have any family members or friends around him as he suffered on that wooden tree. But, there were also several soldiers giving much attention to this man as they awaited his death. I could almost hear this man on the center cross cry out to one of the women who was weeping and groaning in sorrow at the foot of his cross, *'Woman, behold thy son."* (John 19:26 AKJV). In my mind, I could also hear him as he says to one of the men, who was also sorrowing at the foot of his cross, *"Behold thy mother."* (John 19:27 AKJV). This man was dying, but in the midst of his suffering, he took the time to assure that his mother would be in good hands with loving care. According to the Scriptures, Jesus was asking his trusted disciple John to take care of his grieving mother, Mary, while He was preparing to give His life on that cross. (John 19 AKJV)

At this point, my mind fast forwarded a couple of centuries from this scene to a similar scene with another mother and son. I remembered myself as I sat on one side of a thick glass window, talking with my son over a telephone, while he sat on the other side of that same thick glass window. I recalled what my son had said to me as I talked with him concerning my plans to appeal the mandatory ten-year sentence he had been given just a few days before. With a sad, long, pain - filled face, Chris said, *"Momma, don't go broke trying to save me. You have got to live and you don't have much money. I will be alright."* I had no idea, at this point, of

> "O Lord, I don't know how to braid or plat hair!"

God's plan to use my son right where he was, behind prison bars. However, God gave me a peace that I could not understand, through the things that He did that only God could have done. This made me know that my only son was in His hands, and, that he would be alright. My heart continued to ache for my son's situation and the freedom he has lost. However, the more I observed God in the situation, the more peace I experienced. I saw in my own life that *Resurrection Sunday* was the culmination of a dark weekend of events that God's ONLY Son had endured for whoever would believe on Him. *MY ONLY SON* had been given the opprotunity to reach many indivuals, behind prison bars, and lead them to *GOD'S ONLY SON,* even though this opportunity came during what looked like his darkest moments. What was a mistake, or wrong act in judgment on my son's part turned out to be God's opportunity to arrest him, bless him, and make him a blessing. When I had given birth to my son, I knew then that God would use him for Kingdom building. However, I had no idea that this *'using him'* meant that he and I would endure the kind of pain and agony that we would endure over those ten years of his incarceration.

"Cease, my son to hear instruction that causeth you to err from the Words of Knowledge." Proverbs 19:27 (AKJV)

I always wanted a son. Perhaps some of the reason for this mode of thinking may have been a residue of the culture of the Hebrews in the Bible days, especially in the Old Testament times. It was so important for a woman to have a son that a mother, who had accidentally smothered her infant son while they all slept during the night, was willing to, first try to steal her roommate's living infant son and replace him with her dead child while the roommate slept (I Kings 3:16 - 28). This woman was willing to steal someone else's child so that she would not be childless. It did not seem to matter to her that the child was not biologically hers or that her biological child was actually dead. This illustrated just how strongly the culture of that day valued a woman with a child, and especially a son – a male child. When the dispute of who the living child belonged to, came before wise King Solomon, the mother who had stolen the living baby was willing to see Solomon's order, to cut the living baby in half, carried out. However, unexpectedly to those involved, Solomon's wisdom in this ordeal revealed the real mother. The real mother was willing to allow the other woman to keep the living baby, her baby, rather than see the child cut in half! When King Solomon ordered the living baby to be given to the right mother, the other woman was now not only without a son, but she was also childless. This took away so much of her worth and value as a woman. I don't believe that truly was my reason for wanting a son, however, I knew that I could not do hair for a girl child so a son would be much easier!

> *I spent many moments standing in the doors and staring into those two, now empty bedrooms where my children used to be.*

My first child was a beautiful baby girl, born on Sunday, April 24, 1977, at 3:45 PM, in a very small, rural city in Georgia. I had endured a full twenty-four hours of labor believing that this child was a boy. I don't believe the revealing sonograms that we are afforded today were conducted on a regular bases in that day. Therefore, I had no idea whether may baby was a boy or girl, but I was hoping and even praying for a boy. I recall that I was in so much pain and distress during this labor experience that my doctors sedated me in an effort to assist the labor and delivery process; and, to assure that the baby and I could make it through this ordeal and remain healthy. I have to admit that I was a bit disappointed when the doctor told me that I had a girl. I kept saying to myself, "Oh, Lord. I don't know how to braid or plat her hair. I will always have to get someone else to help keep my baby looking good from head to toe." However, when I saw that beautiful little life, as she was placed in my arms, nothing else mattered. I was totally and completely in love. All I could do was stare at her, at the wonder of it all. I was so fascinated with the fact that I had this new baby that I became overwhelmed and cried for several days. They called it post-partum blues, but in my mind I was scared out of my wits of taking care of this little life. I made it through the tough times to say the least, and, almost eight years later, after a full day and night of a very difficult and painful labor, my son was born in Augusta, GA, my hometown. On the morning of February 20, 1985, at precisely 8:05 AM, I gave birth to a son, a beautiful, handsome baby boy, destined for great things for the Lord, I declared. I had made that declaration over both of my children and I still hold fast to that belief.

Following two failed marriages, I had found myself raising both of my children by myself with the help of God, my mother, and my brothers. I didn't think that my son missed having his father in the home until I read his writings during the development of this publication. My brothers spent a lot of time with 'Chris', as we called my son, especially my brother Walter, who is two years older than I. My children knew my brother Walter as 'Uncle Pop' because all of the family members all called him just that, 'Pop'. Uncle Pop loved to go fishing and would frequently take Chris with him. He even purchased a child sized fishing rod and tackle box set for Chris. I could not believe it when he actually bought that entire child sized tackle box just for Chris. There were times that they would go fishing all day long and even though they many times didn't catch much of anything, Christ enjoyed being with Uncle Pop. I remember having to go and get Chris one Saturday from their favorite fishing spot. Chris was dirty from head to toe, but he absolutely did not want to leave that place and uncle Pop. I almost had to drag him away screaming and crying.

When my daughter went off to college, I missed her so much, but I still had ten year old Chris at home. I believe that, having Chris at home, made seeing her leave a bit easier. However, when I took Chris to college about seven years later, I could hardly make it to my car when it was time to leave without breaking down and I did not want him to see me cry. I believe that at the exact moment that I closed my car door, knowing that I was leaving him, I completely broke down in tears. My baby, my son was now in college, away from home, away from me. I could hardly believe it! Was this what the *empty nest syndrome* felt like? Was this a scary confirmation that I was actually aging? Or, was it just that my son was now gone and I was definitely all alone? All I remember is that I cried most of the four hour trip back home to that empty house. I spent many moments standing and looking into both of those empty rooms.

> *I had no idea the hell we were about experience and that it would last the next ten years!*

With both my children grown up and gone, I drowned my loneliness in the activities of my ministry at the church and in the community. However, it was not long before I realized that God was up to something. That growing discernment that things were about to change again began to overwhelm me. I had come to recognize the feeling that I believe God had given me in prior times to definitely indicate that my purpose at a church was coming to a close. It was not long before I was relocated from the church in Central, Georgia, approximately forty-five miles South of Augusta, Georgia; and, assigned to a church in North Georgia, about twenty-three miles North of Atlanta. When Chris returned home from his freshman year in college, he came to a totally new situation in another city altogether, with new people and new surroundings! He found himself with a totally new group of young people and adults with whom he was now to interact and worship.

Chris was at home only about six weeks during the summer of 2004, the year that we both found ourselves in a totally different ministry situation. He had participated in several capacities in the past two churches to which I had been assigned. He had served as one of the Children Sermon speakers and a Youth Usher. When we came to the church in North Georgia, he almost immediately became a part of the Youth Ushers' Ministry where he met and worked in the church with a young man by the name of Allen. Chris and Allen immediately became friends at church and hung out together a couple of times outside of the church. I don't recall Chris being out many times as he got to know the other youth in the church and the new geographic area. During the first week of August, I took him back to school in South, Georgia for his sophomore year. He was excited about being back in school and back on campus. He got a job in a restaurant on campus, against my wishes. I wanted him to focus on his academics while he saw the need to have more spending money for dates and 'other extra-curricular activities', as he put it. To my surprise, working didn't have much of an effect on his grades. For that, I was more than thankful to Almighty God.

During his sophomore year, Chris came home one time, in the month of October, so that he could pick up the truck that I had purchased for him from one of the members of the congregation. He spent the night and drove the truck back to campus the next morning, four hours away. He didn't come home for Thanksgiving because, as he stated, he wanted to stay on campus so that he could work a few

> *I became hysterical as I screamed, "Yes! ...What has he done?!"*

hours at the restaurant and study for upcoming final exams. Also, during the month of October, Allen, the young man that Chris had worked with on the youth ushers' ministry at the church, had run away from home. After I had attempted, to no avail, to talk with Allen and encourage him to return home to his family, I asked Chris if he would talk with him. My thought was that perhaps Allen might listen to Chris and realize that his family loved him and wanted him home. I sent Allen's mobile number to Chris by text message. However, when Chris arrived home for Christmas on Friday, December 10th, he informed me that he had not spoken with Allen because he had been studying for final exams. Chris further stated that perhaps he would be able to see Allen while he was home for Christmas and that he would speak with him then. At this point, I realized that Chris didn't know this young man extremely well. However, I thought that if perhaps Chris could spend enough time with him, that he might say something to him that would matter and even cause him to change his behavior.

On the first Wednesday evening that Chris was at home for Christmas, he took a young man from the church to Walmart, after Bible study, to get a present for his mother. On his way home, he ran into Allen at one of the neighborhood grocery stores near our apartment home. After making plans to come to the apartment where Allen was living with one of his friends the next day, Chris took the other young man home and returned home himself. Chris told me that he had seen Allen because he knew that I was concerned about him. He also informed me that he and Allen had made plans to talk the next day. I felt sure that once Chris had seen this young man and had an opportunity to talk with him face to face, he would be able to convince Allen to return home. I had no idea that we were headed for a ten- year ordeal as a result of the meeting that had been planned for the following morning. I had no idea the hell we were headed into at that moment. But, I also had no idea the things that God would do, the ways that He would show up just to prove to us that we were important to Him, and, that we were both still in His care.

The next morning, I got up as usual and prepared myself to go to my office at the church. When I noticed that Chris had already gotten up and left home, I was somewhat surprised that he had gotten up and left home so early. Chris was not usually a morning person so this seemed unusual to me. That still, small voice in my spirit was speaking and causing me to take note that this might not be a good thing. But, since I knew that Chris had planned to meet and talk with Allen, I did not allow myself to become alarmed. I called Chris and asked where he was and what he was up to in a light hearted manner with a tiny bit of hidden panic in the background. He assured me that he was okay and that he would be home soon. I don't know why, but I heard myself say to him as if I knew in my spirit that something was up, "You had better not be getting into something you shouldn't. You had better be careful and come home. Talk to Allen and come home. Don't allow yourself to get into any trouble." I didn't really think that there was anything to become upset about since I knew he was supposedly trying to help Allen decide to come back home and get back on the right track. Also, I was trying to get accustomed to the idea that my son was no longer that little boy that I had to keep up with every single moment of the day. However, as the day wore on, I did become more and more upset because I had not heard a word from Chris all day. I went home several times thinking that perhaps he had returned home but just had not called me. The 'not having called me' all day was also not like Chris. Even when he was four hours away in school, not a single day went by that I did not hear from him at least twice. He would call me, whether in the same city or away, at least twice if only to say, "Hello Ma. What are you doing?" To make this more of a concern, one of the members of the church had stopped by the office to ask if we had heard about the attempted bank robbery at the bank in the shopping center right down the street from the church. I had gone shopping earlier in the morning prior to coming to the office and had passed right by the shopping center wondering what was happening that the police cars were there. Never, did I imagine that my son was a part of that frightening looking situation.

Around 5:00PM, the same church member, who had called earlier, called to inform me that my son's friend, who was also a member of the church, had been one of the young men who had attempted to rob the bank. To make matters worse, he had been shot by the policeman in an effort to get him to stop running when he emerged from the bank. I called his parents and found out that they were at a nearby hospital where he had been taken for treatment. Immediately, I got into my car and went to the hospital to be with them. I still had no idea that my son was involved. We were told that my son's friend had been treated and sent to a center where he would be detained for now. All day long, I had continued to call Chris on his cell phone to no avail. When I found out what had happened with that young man, I really became concerned because I already knew deep in my spirit that somehow Chris had been with him. I had this rock in the pit of my stomach that caused me to feel that something was terribly wrong. I started calling the area hospitals to see if Chris was there and had not called me. Finally, I got enough courage to call the County Detention Center (CDC) to ask if my son was there by any strange reason. When a woman answered the phone at the CDC, I asked if by any chance they had Christopher Watkins. The woman said "Hold on a moment." When she returned to the phone and asked, "Do you mean 'Christopher Randolph Watkins?'" I became almost hysterical as I screamed, "Yes! What are you holding him for? What has he done?" Then came the words that pierced my heart through to my spine. I will never forget the woman's words that evening. "He was arrested for armed robbery!" she said. I don't remember if I said thank you or goodbye, or, how I even ended that call and dialed the next. I just remember screaming and crying as I sat in my car in the parking lot of the grocery store. I never made it into the store. Instead, I called Claudia, the congregation member that had given me all the information during the day, and I asked her if she would go to the CDC with me. When I told her that Chris had been one of the young men in that attempted bank robbery earlier that day, she said, "Let's go up there and see if we can see him so we can beat him down." She met me at the church and she drove me to the CDC because I was in no condition to drive anything anywhere.

I was at a complete loss in this situation. I did not know what to do or what to expect! I had never had any legal problems with Chris or anyone else before this. As far as I knew, when it came to the police and law enforcement, Chris was afraid of his shadow! I kept asking myself, "How could this have happened? What could I have done to have avoided this?" We were informed that we would not be able to see Chris or the other young man, but we could attend their first appearance before the judge following morning at the CDC. At this point, we returned to the church where several other church members, who had heard the news concerning the young men, were waiting for us to join them in a prayer session on. The events of the day were not yet real to any of us, but we knew the best thing to do was to pray. I recall as I was kneeling at the altar during this emergency prayer meeting, one of the preachers on staff at the church came over to me and said, "Pastor, the Holy Spirit is telling me that the enemy will try to convince you not to go back into the pulpit and preach because of what has happened." When I heard this statement, I began to understand that there is such a thing as 'holy anger'! I became so angry that I actually felt something rise up on the insde of me so profooundly that it caused me to stand up from my knees. At that point, I heard myself say, "THE DEVIL IS A LIAR! If I have ever preached, you had better believe that I am really going to preach now! The enemy has messed with the right one this time. This will NOT stop me from doing anything the Lord has called me to do! This only fuels my fire for the Lord!" The whole group began to shout praises to the Lord and 'Amen' in agreement to what I had just declared. And I meant every word of it!

While I know that the preacher who had made this statement had meant well, and was trying to warn me of a possible trick of the enemy, I somehow knew, without even knowing that I knew, that God had a larger plan and purpose for all that was happening. And, sure enough, the revelations that I received for sermons and teachings around this entire situation, coupled with God's Word, that began to pour into me for me to pour out to the people were phenomenal! There were so many times that I would prepare a sermon to preach, but the sermon that was delievered was so much more powerful that I could not believe it when I reviewed the notes that I had on paper. There were so many worship experiences where I could not see clearly because of what I believe was the cloud or smoke of the presence of God's Holy Spirit in the sanctuary. In that first year of my son's incarceration, two hundred and forty-nine individuals gave their lives to Christ in that ministry on Sunday during worship alone. That does not include the other times ministry components of the church sponsored events and witnessing was done. I remember one Sunday, after preaching and ending the sermon with a testimony of what God was doing in and through my son, twenty-two people, lead by an eleven year old boy, converged on the little altar of the church, all at once, to give their lives to Christ and to become members of the church. I believe that some individuals in the community who had heard about the bank robbery and my son's involvement, came just to see this pastor who was not ashamed to talk about the situation and testify concerning the move of God with her incarcerated son. Some of theses same people, who had come *just to see*, ended up giving their lives to Christ or joining and working in the ministry of the church.

Just as we had been instructed by the officer on duty, Claudia and I arrived at the CDC the following morning where the young men were to have their first appearance before the judge. We were ushered into this small room where we were able to observe the proceedings from behind a thick glass window that was half the wall. I was absolutely devastated when I saw my son marched into the room, dressed in the orange jail outfit, and stood next to those huge men – and handcuffed! These three boys, looked like toddlers standing there next to those men. I was so distraught that I did not know what to do. My heart was so heavy, I truly thought that it would fall out of my chest! The best thing, and the only thing I knew to do in this situation, I began to do; and that was, I prayed; and, I prayed; and, I prayed. This was my child, my younger child, my baby, and now he is in jail and may be going to prison! Lord, please help me! Lord, PLEASE protect my child in that place. But Lord, PLEASE, BRING HIM OUT?! THIS IS MY ONLY SON!

❖❖❖

SEEING THE HAND OF GOD

"...I will be with thee; I will not fail thee nor forsake thee." Joshua 1:8 (AKJV)

I collected the information on visiting hours and was at the facility on the first day and time that I was told that I would able to visit my son.

> *...God said to me, "You asked me to protect him. You can't tell me how to do it."*

When I arrived to sign in for visitation, I was informed that Chris was on *"Administrative Confinement"* and was not allowed to have visitors at this time. I once again became upset and asked why my son was in confinement with one of the other two young men; and, to make things sound even worse, they informed me that my son would only have thirty minutes a day outside of the cell that he was in. At that point, I was assured by the desk clerk that he should only be in Administrative Confinement two or three days. She explained that this was standard procedure as he is evaluated to determine the best placement for him inside the CDC. That's what the clerk at CDC said to me, but God said, *"You asked me to **protect** him. You can't tell me how to do it."* When I heard this, it was just as real as if someone standing beside me had said it. Later that day, as I was telling Claudia about Chris' confinement, she said in confirmation, "Well Pastor, you did ask God to protect him. Perhaps this is His way of doing it." I was floored when she said that to me. Immediately I remembered the scripture in that says, "In the mouth of two or three witnesses shall everything be established."(2 Corinthians 13:1b) I told Claudia that this was exactly what God had spoken to me as I whined to Him about Chris being locked up within the Administrative Confinement!

I went ahead and began to take care of things for Chris, such as retaining a lawyer, withdrawing him from school, going to campus to get his things; and, calling his supervisor at the restaurant to inform her that he would not be returning. When I spoke with Chris' supervisor at the restaurant, she said, "Oh, my goodness, what am I going to do? He was my best worker!" I didn't go into detail as to what the situation entailed. I had not yet gotten to the point of accepting what was actually happening in our lives. I could not discuss the situation with anyone because for me it was still surreal. I was praying silently that I was going to wake up at any moment and find that this had all been an awful dream.

I had been informed, when Chris was initially incarcerated, that he would probably be in Administrative Confinement for only two or three days. At the end of two and a half months, Chris said to me one day, "Mama, I think they are going to take me out of here and put me in population tomorrow." My heart sank like a ton of bricks had just been dropped inside of it. This meant that Chris would now have to interact with all of the other inmates in the area where he was assigned. I cannot even explain or express how concerned I was for him in this "God-awful" place, I thought, with no protection. All day long that

> *"Oh my goodness", she said! "...He was my best worker!"*

day I prayed, more frequently than usual, and I asked God to intervene on my son's behalf. I absolutely did not want him in population. While I had no idea what, if any, other options were available for my child, all I could remember was seeing those huge men and those little boys side by side on the day of their first appearance. My mind began to imagine some of the most horrible things happening to my child behind bars in a situation where he may not have been able to defend himself or have anyone who would come to his aid. I remember that when I laid my head on my pillow that night, I said to God, "Lord, I can't do a thing about Chris' situation, but I know that You can. Lord, You have people everywhere, even behind prison bars. Please, surround him with people who will help him and not try to take advantage of him; people who will pray with him and for him; Christian people who will help get the Word in him." I remember that it was not twenty – four hours later that Chris called my mother because he could not get me. I was not at home and mobile phones had not yet been allowed on the phone list for inmates. As I was driving down a busy road in Atlanta, my mother called me and said, "Chris called me a little while ago because he could not get you. They did take him out of confinement today," my mother said while my heart got that heavy feeling again. But, to my surprise, my mother continued with these words. "While he was talking with me, he put this man on the phone and the man said, 'Ma'am, I know you are worried about your grandson, but don't worry about him. He is in here with people who will help him and not take advantage of him. He's with Christians who will study with him..." Every word I had said to God the night before, that man had said to my mother, and, she repeated to me on the phone that afternoon as if she had heard my conversation with God the night before. I was so excited and moved by this confirmation that God had heard my prayer that I had to pull over off the road so that I could pray and praise the Lord! I was driving the truck I had bought for Chris and was so filled with praise that it took me a while to drive home. God had not only heard but He had answered my prayers. I had no idea who the man was with Chris, but I had God's assurance that my son was in the hands of someone who belonged to the Lord.

A few months later, the same man who had spoken to my mother with Chris that afternoon had been released from the CDC, found my church and became a hard working member of the church. He told me the story of his first meeting with Chris inside the jail. He said that the minute my son had walked through the door into the population area of the jail where he was to be placed, the Holy Spirit said to him, "That young man does not belong in here. Watch out for him and take care of him. He is here in preparation to fulfill **MY** purpose for his life." He said that he went over to Chris and immediately began to take him under his wing and help him with getting acclimated to life on the inside. I believe that this man was there for a purpose as well. I believe that God had this man positioned just where and when needed, so that he would be able to help my son as he learned the things he needed to know in order to navigate prison life. This man was a Christian and my son had ten long years ahead of him and he needed to be reminded of the Goodness of the Lord as well as understand the do's and don'ts of prison life.

I entered seminary in Atlanta, and I volunteered to do one of my class internships at a nearby women's prison. While I was there working with the women and researching for papers, I learned so much concerning incarceration in this country and especially in the State of Georgia. It was then that the term "Mass Incarceration" became a meaningful part of my vocabulary. Because of news reports here and there and an occasional newspaper or magazine headline, I had been made aware of the fact that the population of inmates in the United States was growing at a rate faster than that of other countries; and, that there was definitely not equality when it came to the races and genders of the individuals who are incarcerated each year. I was vaguely aware that African Americans and Latinos were incarcerated at rates much higher than Caucasians. When I observed the many groups inside the women's prison as they were on their way to the dining hall; and or, as they attended the worship services when I came to preach, I felt that the crowds and groups confirmed the numbers and inequality I had heard and read about.

> *On Monday, January 24, 2011, at approximately 8:00 AM, my mother passed away in Augusta, GA.*

I was excited to have the opportunity to volunteer inside of a prison so that I could also gain a better idea of what life is actually like for the average inmate in the state of Georgia. I learned so much concerning the life of the incarcerated individuals, and, as my son and I talked and compared notes, it seemed that his life was just about the same as what I was seeing in the women's prison. When I learned about the Faith and Character Program along with the Faith and Character residence inside the women's prison, I couldn't wait to check with my son concerning the State prison where he was now housed in South Georgia. My son confirmed that the same program was indeed offered at the prison where he was assigned. I was so tempted to call and ask the chaplain at that state prison and ask if my son could be considered for this Faith and Character program and the dorm placement. However, every time I thought about calling to ask about this, I distinctly heard the Holy Spirit say, "No. Don't Call." On several occasions, I actually picked up the phone to call the chaplain and heard the Holy Spirit say, "No." I didn't understand why I was not to call and make this request on behalf of my son, but I obeyed the Holy Spirit and prayed that God would move on his behalf if this program was for him.

On Monday, January 24, 2011, at approximately 8:00 AM, my mother passed away in Augusta, GA. Although my mother was in a nursing home due to her need for twenty – four hour medical care, her death was not expected. She seemed to have been doing well. I had spoken with her on the afternoon before. My mother and my son Chris had been so very close that she was the one person in my family that I did had dreaded having to tell that he had been arrested and even accused of doing wrong. My mother had been Chris' babysitter from the time that he was about eight weeks old until he went to pre-school at four years of age. After Chris started pre-school, my mother continued to keep him and my daughter while I worked in the evenings and sometimes when I worked on weekends. By the time Chris started pre-school, I was divorced with just my children and myself in my home. Secretly, I had been praying that my mother would live to see Chris come home with his freedom from incarceration. Although

> *I was hurt and I wanted to quip back something... immediately the Holy Spirit said, "Don't say a Word!"*

Chris and I had not talked about it, the Holy Spirit had placed it on my heart that Chris and my mother were both praying for the same thing. Therefore, it was very difficult for me to think that my mother would not be there to see Chris freed and come home. As much as I had dreaded having to tell my mother about Chris' situation, I dreaded just as much having to tell Chris that my mother had passed away. I knew that he would have a difficult time accepting this news.

When I called the Chaplain at the State Prison to ask him to speak with Chris and let him know what had happened, I wanted him to understand that this would be difficult for Chris because of the kind of closeness that he and his grandmother had shared. The Chaplain stated to me without any compassion, "They don't think about things like that when they do things and get themselves in trouble and in places like this." I was so hurt when he said that to me, and I wanted to quip back something at him in response and in defense of my son, but I immediately heard the Holy Spirit say, "Don't say a word!" I quietly and hesitantly asked him if he could call me when he had Chris in his office so that I could speak with him to see how he was taking the news, and, if he wanted me to work on having him to come home for the funeral services. When the chaplain called me back that afternoon about 1:30 PM, he had Chris with him, but before he gave Chris the phone to speak with me, he said some things to me that I will never forget. He said, "I have talked at length with Chris and I just want you to know that you have a wonderful son. He truly has his head on straight about his life from here on out, and, I don't believe that you will ever have to be concerned about him coming this way again. As a matter of fact, I am going to get him in the Faith and Character program and work it out so that he can be moved to live in the Faith and Character building!" At that moment, I understood clearly why the Lord did not allow me to call the chaplain and request this placement for my son. God wanted to confirm to both of us once again that He was not only in control, but, that He was also still with my child, even behind prison bars.

When my son was a younger child, he would always sit in the back of the church sanctuary as I conducted worship services and preached. I was always so sure that he was not listening to what was happening. I never imagined that he was actually listening to the sermons during worship or the lessons during Bible study or Sunday Church School. Imagine my surprise but extreme pleasure when I received some of the outlines of sermons and Bible study lessons that Chris had been preaching and teaching while he was incarcerated. I could not believe it! He was actually listening and not only listening, but retaining and understanding what he had been hearing! I was not only pleased, I was also so very proud of him. I told him one day how proud I was of him and he was floored! "Proud of me!?" He said in a voice tone that seemed to continue, "How can you be proud of me and I am in this situation, in prison?!" He never actually voiced that thinking, but I could tell that was exactly what he was thinking. "Yes!" I said. "I am very proud of the mindset that you have taken because I realize that you could have gone in a totally opposite direction with this incarceration. You could have gone in there and been in trouble all of the time. You could have acquired such a negative, defeated attitude, but, instead, you are doing things to honor and glorify God!" I meant what I said, I was so extremely proud of my son for the things that he was doing inside the prison. Of course I was not happy that he was incarcerated, but I was extremely happy that he was Glorifying God in this situation.

> *Yes! I am proud of you... you are doing things to honor and glorify God.*

I recall Chris telling me about the overwhelming numbers of African American males who were incarcerated in the same facility with him. He was also truly alarmed by the apparently low academic levels of the majority of the inmates with whom he found himself interacting. Chris said that when he started talking about concepts like fractions, it was as if he was speaking French to many of the fellow inmates in the facility. Their knowledge and understanding seemed so limited and lacking. Chris said that he constantly found himself tutoring and teaching the other inmates in various academic areas. My advice to him is to help whenever he had the opportunity because the research that I had been conducting, during my classes in Seminary, had revealed quite a few facts concerning incarceration that had truly surprised me.

According to Emily B. Nichols and Ann B. Loper, in their November 2012 article published in the *Journal of Youth and Adolescence*, the United States has the highest incarceration rate in the world. Yet, there is relatively little information on how the removal of these adults from the home to incarceration impacts the youth and children who are left behind.[1] They found that the youth who had experienced the incarceration of a household member were more likely to report extended absences from school, and, were less likely to graduate from high school relative to those youth who did not experience a household member's incarceration. Youth who had experienced the incarceration of a household member evidenced more socioeconomic challenges, more frequent home adversities; and, lower cognitive skills relative to youth who did not experience the incarceration of a household member.

In 1997, seventeen years ago, Walter Wenda reported that non-Caucasian males made up approximately 50% of the U.S. prison population. He further stated that African Americans are incarcerated in the United States at a rate *four times* that of South Africans when Apartheid was legal.[2] There was, however, very little documentation or research on how the removal of a

---

[1]   Emily B. Nichols & Ann B. Loper. Incarceration in the Household: Academic Outcomes of Adolescents with an Incarcerated Household Member. *Journal of Youth and Adolescence*. V41, n11, p1455 – 1471, November 2012

[2]   Walter Wenda. The Relationship Between Life Skills-Literacy and Vocational Education and the Self-Perception of Eleven domains and global Self Worth of Adult Incarcerated Males. *Journal of Correctional Education*. March 1997. V48, Issue 1. P24 – 29.

youth from the home to incarceration impacts the mother, the father, and/or the other siblings and family members that may also be an integral part of that family. In an April 2012 article published by the *American Sociological Review*, Christopher Wildeman, Jason Schnittker and Kristin Turney stated that while there is plenty of research which considers the consequences of mass incarceration on adult males, 'Yet virtually no quantitative research considers the consequences of *mass imprisonment* for the well-being of the women who are the link between the prisoners or former prisoners and their children who are left behind'.[3]

The following is a further sampling of the kind of research examined concerning children with incarcerated parents:

- Michael E. Roettger and Raymond R. Swisher examined 'The Association of Father's History of Incarceration with the son's Delinquency and Arrest among Black, White and Hispanic Males in the United States', in a November 2011 article published by *Criminology*. These researchers found that a father's incarceration is highly and significantly associated with an *increased risk* of the son incurring an adult arrest before 25 years of age. These observed associations were similar across groups of Black, White and Hispanic males.[4]
- In December 2012, Jean Kjellstrand, Jennifer Cearley, Mark J. Eddy, Dana Foney, and Charles Martinez reported that the number of children of incarcerated parents in the U.S. has grown dramatically in recent years.[5]

[3]   Christopher Wildeman, Jason Schnittker, & Kristin Turney. Despair by Association? The Mental Health of Mothers with Children by Recently Incarcerated Fathers. *American Sociological Review.* April 2012, v77, Issue 2, p.216 - 243

[4]   Michael E. Roettger & Raymond R. Swisher. Associations of Father's History of Incarceration with Son's Delinquency and Arrest Among Black, White, and Hispanic Males in the United States. *Criminology.* November 2011, v49, Issue 4, p1109 - 1147

[5]   Jean Kjellstrand, Jennifer Cearley, Mark Eddy, Dana Foney, and, Charles Martinez. Characteristics of Incarcerated Fathers and Mother: Implications for Preventive Interventions Targeting Children an Families. Children and Youth Services Review. December 2012. V34. Issue 12. P2409 – 2416.

- Danielle H. Dallaire found that incarcerated mothers represent a rapidly growing sector of the prison population. She reported that academic difficulties for school aged children, and, risky behaviors that may place adolescent children at increased risk for incarceration themselves resulted when mothers were incarcerated.[6] The problem is, most of the researchers seemed to disagree as to whether or not it was the father or the mother that was incarcerated more frequently.

- Increases in the population of incarcerated women in the U.S. have resulted in the separation of growing numbers of mothers and children. The negative effects of dividing families have been noted for both mothers and children. Researcher Zoann K. Snyder utilized a frequent visitation program for keeping incarcerated mothers and their children together and found very positive results for both the mothers and the children.[7]

- Julie Poehlmann reported that the mother – child relationships were more positive when incarcerated mothers had more frequent telephone contact with older children. She also asserted, in this September 2005 article published in the *Journal of Family Psychology*, that the quality of the mother – caregiver relationships should be a point of consideration. According to Poehlmann, the more negative the mother – caregiver relationship, the less likely the mother is to have frequent visits with the child.[8]

- Author Keva M. Miller reported that African American children are the most greatly impacted by this social issue as they account for over 50% of all children of incarcerated parents in the United States. They are negatively responding to the parent – child

---

[6]   Danielle H. Dallaire. Children With Incarcerated Mothers: Developmental Outcomes, Special Challenges and Recommendations. *Journal of Applied Developmental Psychology*. Jan-Feb. 2007. V28.n1.p15 - 24

[7]   Zoann K. Snyder. Keeping Families Together: The Importance of Maintaining Mother – Child contact for Incarcerated Women. *Women & Criminal Justice*. Jan – March 2009. V19. Issue 1. P37 – 59.

[8]   Julie Poehlmann. Incarcerated Mothers' Contact With Children, Perceived Family Relationships, and Depressive Symptoms. *Journal of Family Psychology*. V19 (3). September 2005. P350 – 357.

separation due to the incarceration; and, are vulnerable to a myriad of adverse psychological, emotional, and behavioral outcomes.[9]

- In his January-April 2012 article, author Chang-Bae Lee found that though serving lengthy sentences, a significant percentage of the 185 incarcerated fathers in his study valued a positive father – child relationship.[10]

Joby Gardner, in an April 2010 study of incarcerated young men published in *Youth and Society*, stated that working – class Brown and Black young men face very difficult transitions, as they are overrepresented in the justice system, in poverty statistics, in foster care, special education; and, among victims of violence.[11] In spite of the scarcity of documented research or other information concerning mothers of incarcerated children, perhaps the design for a plan of support for mothers should draw on information and research presented in examining the challenges mothers and children experience from the incarceration of mothers or fathers. Any design to support and meet the needs of a mother who is experiencing the incarceration of a child should definitely seek to meet the needs of not only the mother, but also the incarcerated child as well as the other siblings; and, the father if he is present.

Patrick Seffrin from Bowling Green State University conducted a longitudinal study of 197 juvenile delinquents and reported in October 2006, that, although Whites reported significantly higher levels of delinquency than Blacks during adolescence, the trend reverses in adulthood. According to Seffrin, factors such as employment, marriage, educational abilities; and, neighborhoods all contribute to the stability or instability of a former juvenile delinquent. He further reported that the effects of a negative neighborhood context was significant for Blacks only.

---

[9]   Keva M. Miller. Risk and Resilience Among African American Children of Incarcerated Parents. *Journal of Human Behavior in the Social Environment.* 2007. V15, Issue 2/3. P25 – 37.

[10]   Chang-Bae Lee, Frank A, Sansone, Cheryl Swanson, & Kimberly M. Tatum. Incarcerated Fathers and Parenting: Importance of the Relationship with their Children. *Social Work in Public Health.* Jan – Apr 2012. Vol. 27. Issue ½. P.165 - 186

[11]   Joby Gardner. Beyond "Making It" or Not: Future Talk by Incarcerated Young Men. *Urban Education.* V45 N1. P75 - 102

[12] Perhaps this speaks not only to the idea of the family dynamics, but also the idea of how we relate to one another beyond the nuclear family. One question we may need to ask is what our neighborhood family dynamics look like. My mother, grandmother and even I, myself, recall a time when neighbors were more of an extended family than they are now. Are we no longer our brother's keeper in the African American community?

Mary Ann Zehr examined the Maya Angelou Academy which, in November 2010, was serving 60 – 70 incarcerated teenagers from 14 to 19 years of age. She found that nationwide, experts report that top – notch educational services for incarcerated young people are a rarity.[13] David Domenici, Principal of the Maya Angelou Charter School for incarcerated youth, said that this is one of the few programs in the country attempting to improve the quality of educational services to incarcerated youth. It is in a pocket of a field that many agree has been largely ignored. However, he states that at Maya Angelou he has teachers that like the students and don't make fun of them if they can't read but passionately try to help them.[14]

In their March 2001 article, published in the *Journal of Correctional Education*, Cathy Gilham and Barbara Moody discussed another strategy for improving the quality of educational services to incarcerated youth in the U.S. They examined a 'video – conferencing' strategy using desktop computers at Robert Farrell School in Oregon. As they discussed, this strategy could help to advance a Distance Learning Programs methodology in the various facilities where our youth are housed. A Distance Learning Methodology could help to improve the quality of education to our youth behind bars while at the same time serve to connect them to the outside community.[15]

Kathryn Monahan, Asha Goldweber, & Elizabeth Cauffman investigated the impact of visitations from parents on the mental and

---

[12] Patrick Seffrin. An Examination of black-White Crime Differences in a Sample of Previously Incarcerated Youth: Does Neighborhood Context Explain the Race Gap in Adult Crime? *Bowling Green State University/OhioLink 2006-10-17*

[13] Mary Ann Zehr. Academy Engages Incarcerated Youth. Education Week. V30. N11. November 2010. P1, 14 – 15.

[14] Ibid.

[15] Cathy Gilham & Barbara Moody. Face to Face: Video Conferencing Creates Opportunities for Incarcerated Youth. Journal of Correctional Education. Mar2001. Vol.52 Issue 1. P29

emotional health of incarcerated youth in a secure juvenile facility. The results indicated that youth who receive visits from parents report a more rapid decline in depressive symptoms over time compared to youth who do not receive visits from parents. They further reported that these results were cumulative such that the greater the number of visits from parents, the greater the decrease in depressive symptoms.[16]

In her March 2011 article published in *Urban Review*, Joby Gardner found that incarcerated young men and their supervisors talked about faith as a force for positive change in their lives. She asserts that faith represents a potential asset in efforts to assist incarcerated young offenders as they pursue education, legal work, and sobriety. According to Gardner, religious affiliation, and spirituality more generally, are protective and can promote other positive developmental outcomes. Moreover, Gardner suggests that critically exploring matters of faith and belief in public institutions might prove useful in informing curricular and programmatic interventions to assist young people in avoiding recidivism, school failure, and substance abuse; and, perhaps, find or imagine satisfying and meaningful adult lives.[17]

From my personal experience with the Corrections System of this country, I have witnessed many of the aspects in which incarceration has become big business. Very little of the money raised on the backs of our loved ones is used to benefit our loved ones or their families, in spite of the fact that Federal and State Tax dollars are also earmarked for the Corrections System.

---

[16] Kathryn Monahan, Asha Goldweber, & Elizabeth Cauffman. The Effects of Visitation on Incarcerated Juvenile Offenders: How Contact with the Outside Impacts Adjustment on the Inside. Law and Human Behavior. April 2011. Vol. 35. Issue 2. P143 – 151.

[17] Joby Gardner. Keeping Faith: Faith Talk by and for Incarcerated Youth. *Urban Review: Issues and Ideas in Public Education.* March 2011. V43 n1 p22 – 42.

GOD IS STILL ON HIS THRONE: AND HE IS STILL WORKING THINGS OUT!

"And we know that all things work together for good to them that love God, to them that are the called according to His purpose." Romans 8:28 (AKJV)

While incarcerated at the State Prison in South, GA, Chris had been informed that because of his charges of armed robbery, he would not qualify for a Transitional Housing placement outside of the facility. This type of placement would allow him to live in the community, away from the prison facility, and, be able to acquire a job in the community. The staff of the Transitional Home would be responsible for assisting Chris in getting a job and making sure he was transported to and from his job so that he could work. He would, of course, earn a salary, but would not be able to keep all of the money he earned. An account had been established for Chris upon entering the Georgia Prison system so that I could send money to him for his basic necessities, since he could not work on a paying job inside the prison. It was to this account that I had tried to make sure he had money so that he could purchase the necessary items that were sold at each of the facilities to which he had been assigned during his incarceration. I had learned from my time as a volunteer in the women's prison near Atlanta that inmates don't always receive the bare necessities such as soap, toothpaste, etc. unless they had enough money in their accounts to purchase these items from the facility store.

Of course, I, and my prayer warrior friends, took this denial of Transitional placement to the Lord in prayer, believing that God would work it out so that Chris would be given a Transitional Center placement. We prayed that God would bless Chris to be able to receive a placement in a Transitional Home in spite of what the law said. I believed and continued to speak that God will change the law for those who belonged to Him. And guess what! God did it! God changed the law!

One extremely cold and rainy day in January of 2014, I had stopped to get gas after leaving my seminary class in Atlanta when I received a call from Chris. When I answered, I could tell that Chris rather happy about something as he said, "Mama, guess where I am!" I could tell that he was excited but I had no idea what to answer. "Where?!" I answered. He excitedly replied, "I am at the Transitional Center in South, GA!" The first words out of my mouth were, "Praise the Lord!" I knew without a shadow of a doubt that it had to have been God moving on the hearts and minds of those in charge of my son and allowing him this opportunity to transition back into society. After a few weeks in the center, Chris was still not able to receive a job and was becoming somewhat anxious about it.

> *God did it! God changed the law!*

At this point, things took what appeared to be a downward turn at the Transitional center in South Georgia,. Chris became so enraged one evening, when he was not allowed to go shopping, that he ended up in lockdown. Because he was not allowed to go shopping for necessary toiletries with the other inmates, Chris saw this as the final straw to what had been a string of unfair denials he had received. He protested with loud, extreme behavior and ended up in lockdown. As he described it, "I couldn't help it. I had had it! I cursed everybody out!" When it was time for his hearing the next day, an officer from the state level just happened to be present and observed the hearing. Although Chris had told the officers that he had nothing to say, he said that the Holy Spirit told him to speak. When he described the kind of treatment that he and the others had been receiving, the state officer was extremely attentive to what he was saying. This fueled his desire to tell everything! He told the presiding officer that if he could not get the necessary toiletries to take care of himself and he could not get a job, send him back to prison. He was informed that if he went back to prison, it could be three months before he would be able to be considered for another Transitional placement. When he stated that he was okay with this, however, if the center in South Georgia was the only place that he could be sent, his request still stands to go back to prison; the state officer sat up in her seat. As he was escorted out of the room, the state officer called to him and gestured what appeared to say that she was looking out for him. Coincidence? I don't think so because we don't serve a coincidental God. The next day, Chris called me again and said, "Guess where I am!" I had no idea. Then I heard him say, "I am at the Augusta Transitional Center!" I was so excited! He was at home, in my own hometown! This was no one but God moving on Chris' behalf! He was in Augusta, GA! He was at home! My brother and sister-in-law were both in Augusta. He was close to family, praise the Lord!

On December 16, 2014, exactly ten years after that awful day on December 16, 2004 when Chris was arrested, I went home to Augusta, GA to walk my child out of incarceration. For me, this was truly a culmination of events that helped me better understand God's way of using us. What a blessed day it was. He now lives in my mother's home, is working two jobs, and, is preparing to go back to school and finish his degree. God is still working on his behalf. Every academic credit he had will still count; and, the Governor of Georgia changed the law that felons can receive the Nathan Deal Grant, which was formerly the Hope Grant, for school. What a Mighty God we serve. He is blessing my only son just as He blessed us over 2,000 years ago through HIS ONLY SON! All that I had endured with my son's incarceration reminded me of seeing Mary at the foot of the cross as her Son and God's ONLY Son were sacrificed on the cross so that anyone who would believe on Jesus Christ could have eternal life. My son had spent ten years in s state prison where he had a tutor, teacher, preacher and Christian counselor to so many young men behind bars. Ten years of his life were sacrificed for countless others just as Christ sacrificed for 'whosoever will come to Him'.

PART TWO

VALUABLE LIFE LESSONS
LEARNED...
THE HARD WAY!

VALUABLE LIFE LESSONS LEARNED...
THE HARD WAY!

INTRODUCTION

I would first like to thank you for the fact that you are not only holding this book in your hand, but you are also reading its contents. Perhaps you purchased this book from your favorite bookstore, website; or, perhaps you are the recipient of a blessing from a thoughtful friend or associate. How you obtained this writing is totally irrelevant. What is important to me, however, is that I truly believe that you will be touched, enlightened, and moved by the messages contained in these pages. My mother used to always say that sometimes God has to *arrest* us in order to be able to **bless** us. I believe that may be some of what happened to me.

I don't consider myself a minister, a Bible scholar or even an expert. I do consider myself young man at thirty years old, which perhaps may make many of you my elders. I don't believe that any of that matters either. What does matter is that my intentions, through this writing, are to help anyone reading the messages of these pages, live a healthy and happy life, see some of the ills of some areas of our society; and, realize that all of us are here for a reason and every experience we have in our lives is for a reason. Because I have come to realize that I have been sick and depressed; and, may be hindered in my future accomplishments as a result of some of the life choices I have made; I would like to help someone else to be able to avoid the same pitfalls and wrong choices. Not only do I desire to get my life back on the right track, but, I also have a strong desire to help someone else find the right path and not ever become lost again.

In Part 1 of this publication, my mother, Rev. Dr. Lugenia Johnson, gave you her perspective and her experiences dealing with the events that took place in my life as a result of having been temporarily derailed. My mother loves the Lord God with all her heart, soul and might, therefore, I truly believe that she has given the reader exactly what God intended. Her words were precise and accurate as she described seeing the Hand of God in every situation. Yet, because she was able to see the Hand of God in every situation, my mother was able to recount the events and experiences from a place of comfort and peace that only God could give. And, I believe that God did give her the peace and comfort that she needed to be able to get through the gut wrenching experience of having 'her only son' locked away in the prison system for ten, long years.

My mother has achieved and become what I perhaps foresee for my future. She is a Pastor, a Scholar, and, I believe an expert in her career fields. She can extract lessons from stories and events that others might never be able to see in a lifetime. My mother is one of the most intelligent people I have ever come in contact with; and, I realize that I am truly blessed to have her as my mother. I, on the other hand, am a work in progress. As yet, I do not possess a college degree from anywhere. People whom I have met have often used the words 'bright' or 'intelligent' to describe me after interacting with me. I believe, however, that these words are like the verb form of the word 'Love' – they are action words. I believe that an individual must be able to demonstrate that he/she loves another by their words and actions towards the other. Likewise, I also believe that intelligence must be demonstrated through the wise choices an individual makes. And, when I consider, some of the choices that I have made in my short life, I believe that my enemy, the devil, is trying to cause me to be hard pressed to believe, at this point, that I am indeed intelligent or bright. So why am I continuing to write? Good question!

> *I, on the other hand, am a work in progress.*

I have experienced a great deal in my young life, and I have learned many lessons. With every lesson learned comes the opportunity to share the trials, tribulations, the stories; and, make a difference in someone else life. History always seems to repeat itself. However, I pray that everyone reading this writing will receive what is needed so that what is now my history does not have to be repeated in anyone's life and definitely not in mine. I believe that every time we come through an experience or situation, we are meant to share it as there may be someone behind us trying to navigate around the same potholes in their lives. Life is difficult enough as it is, and, I don't think there is anyone who could not use a helping hand at some point in life. If God can be a 'Friend that sticks closer than a brother' (Proverbs 18:24 NIV), imagine the relationship we as brothers and sisters, in Christ, should have. I am a brother in Christ desiring to help someone navigate the map of life with my story, my trials and lessons learned to help in decision making. However, I realize that when traveling, not everybody reads the map. The choice is still yours.

---❖❖❖---

10 YEARS OF LESSONS LEARNED: FINDING GOD IN WHAT LOOKED LIKE A HOPELESS SITUATION

And we know that <u>ALL THINGS</u> work together for good to them that love God, to them who are the called according to His purpose. Romans 8:28 (AKJV)

Incarcerated Encouragement
by Christopher R. Watkins

Out of the deepest, darkest abyss I came
Within the brightest beacon of light I reside.
Morphed and molded by the hottest of flames
And on comfy, cozy cushions I lie -
I've been battered and bruised by the biggest of men,
Yet survived to tell the tallest of tales
Of a word where even your closest of kin
Can't save you from savage, sour males!
Everyday you ponder and pray for a change.
Every night you are wishing foe wonderful peace.
Every morning you awake, you arise, and maintain.
Every evening you are thankful you made it, at least -
No cal-very is coming to rescue and retrieve.
No hope for the humble, no hero in sight;
Just a conscience that is calling, urging you to believe...
...That sooner than later everything will be alright.

It took me a year and a half, but I finally learned that I had to deal with my situation or it would deal with me. I had to determine in my heart and mind that I would come out of this situation and that I would come out better, stronger, and wiser than I had gone into it. I had to find the steps to make the most of a horrible place, so I began to write, to teach Bible Study, to tutor others at times, to lead worship; and, to love the Lord, my God with all my heart, with all my soul, and, with all my might. In other words, when I got my focus in the right place, the lessons began to come, but, they became easier and easier to receive and to learn. I asked myself "What are you going to do? What are your next steps?" And in this proverbial death, *I FOUND LIFE*! I came to realize that God truly had a *call* or *purpose* for my life, and, that I had to find my way to accomplish that purpose, even behind prison bars, because in my purpose, I knew, I would find not only *LIFE but ETERNAL LIFE WITH GOD!*

The Journey Begins: Finding And Accepting My Purpose!

At this point in my incarceration, as I am writing this, I was a young, Black man, twenty-eight years of age. I realized that I had traveled a long way in my journey, but yet, I saw that the road continued to stretch quite a distance ahead of me. I consider myself a very humble human being who is mixed with the necessary edge to be taken seriously. I have been told since I was a child that I have been called to preach. While I have not yet accepted this destiny, if this is what is truly meant for me, I realize that perhaps that prophecy may be metaphoric. As I consider the concept of leadership, I realize that a Pastor is the Leader of his/her congregation. Because of this revelation or realization, I have come to acknowledge what looks to me as training possibly leading me in that direction.

When I was a little child, my mind was extremely sharp and I quickly adopted music as my hobby. I was mesmerized by the piano that my mother owned and played. The melody of the eighty -eight keys played in harmonic fashion to this day has a wonderful effect on me. My mother pointed out that I had a skill of what was called "playing by ear", or without notes. With the mental capacity that I possessed, learning to play other instruments also came easily to me. I now realize that learning to the play the instruments and standing before a crowd, giving a performance was leadership training also. My music made it possible for me to demonstrate a skill that not everyone has.

My willingness to speak also kept me before a microphone. It didn't matter if it was an Easter speech or a class presentation, there weren't too many opportunities that I didn't take. I've done so many things from playing the character Romeo, to performing the "I Have A Dream" speech by the Rev. Dr. Martin Luther King, Jr. Although I believe that I should have won, when I was in the eighth grade I was awarded second place in a local essay contest on the subject of "Optimism". While I was at a State Prison in Central, GA, I was the winner of a poetry contest with a poem that I had written titled "My Journey Down 'Life Avenue'". I can even remember how, in fifth grade, I was tricked into singing in a talent show. I had originally gone on stage with my friend during the audition only to help him. However, I ended up singing "Amazing Grace" as a solo. I have Mrs. Martin to thank for that!

> *My only fear was remembering the plays, however, it turned out to be easier than I had anticipted.*

When I was in the eighth grade, I became a part of the Seminole football team. I had never played the position of quarterback before. Because I had been a chubby kid, I had always played lineman in recreational football. But, I had slimmed down and had a "rocket" right arm! My only fear was remembering the plays, however, it turned out to be easier than I had anticipated. Now my questions were, "How would this passionate group of guys respond to my leadership?" "Was I really the man for the job?" The answer came during our game against Hephzibah Middle School.

The game was basically over already and our starters were already on the sideline. Our fire was ignited when what looked like a dirty lick left our back-up quarter back injured and down on the opposition's sideline. My team was ready to fight! I was ready to fight! But, rather than engage in an illegal act that would surely become a brawl between the two teams, I decided to take a different approach to the situation. I entered the game and swiftly gathered the troops in a huddle. "Let's punish them", I urged. Those weren't exactly the words I used, but, they got the message. Refocusing their energy to the task at hand, we proceeded to pound that football down their throats with a ferocity that even shocked me. We didn't even need the touchdown, but, it felt good to cross that line knowing they had absolutely no chance of stopping our drive. I saw first-hand what organized anger could do. It was a beautiful moment. However, this moment demonstrated to me how critical the leader can become to any group.

I remember my first game as the starter quarterback in high school. We were predominantly an <u>option team</u>, but, I was more of a <u>spread quarterback</u>. In the second quarter we had set up nicely for a strike and my coach gave me the green light. When I got to the huddle of players, I remember telling the guys, "Give me three seconds and I promise you a touchdown." As I think back to that moment, that may have been the prettiest pass I had ever thrown in my life. We made the playoffs that year but were overwhelmed in the first round. All in all, I enjoyed every minute of that experience which I now see as training for a leadership role in life as well.

My time of incarceration has been a time of reflection. Many people don't realize it, but, this is the best time for a person to actually meditate on his/her life and the direction they have been taking. When I was arrested in December 2004, I could see no silver lining behind that cloud. Taking time to meditate and reflect was alien to me at that time. My attitude was "What was I going to get out of meditating anyway?" What kind of training could I receive in a prison system that only had GED as an academic possibility, when I had almost completed my sophomore year in college? Within one year, I began to realize that all hope was not lost. I began to do all that I could to expand my present knowledge of the Word of God – the Bible. Before I knew it, I had begun to display a level of maturity that I had never before realized that I possessed. I was ultimately separated from my own age group by way of mental capacity and thought processes. I realized that I just didn't fit in anymore with my own chronological age group. I can't explain what I was beginning to see in myself and demonstrate with others, however, I began to feel it without a shadow of a doubt.

Soon, I found myself in the presence of men of great faith. With these guys, there was no such thing as a "Chained-gang religion" that lasted only while they were incarcerated. When they realized that there was something different about me in spite of how young I was, they welcomed me into their fold with open arms and my development continued. I realize now that *God was not about to allow His plan for my life to be hindered, stolen, or derailed by the* enemy. As the Word of God states, "The gifts and callings of the Lord are without repentance."(Romans 11:29 AKJV). The men in this group helped me to rediscover my confidence, my voice, and my God-given gifts. I could now teach a couple of Bible study sessions.

> *I realize now that God was not about to allow His plan for my life to be hindered, stolen, or derailed by the enemy.*

Each of the three times that I was moved to another penal facility, I was amazed at the youth and young adults that are in the system. Since I felt that I had been "reared" by the system, I felt that I was in a position to share insight with those who were coming behind me. Some listened and some did not. My responsibility and charge, as I comprehended it, was to relay the messages that I believed God had given me for them whenever I had the opportunity. It was always interesting to me to observe that the individuals that needed the information the most were usually in the right place at the right time to receive it. Whether they did actually receive what I had to say, I may never know.

I entered the "Faith and Character Based" Program at the State Prison in March of 2011 and graduated from it the following year in September 2012. Once again, I was placed in a leadership position becoming a *Peer Counselor* for Team 5 of the program. It appeared to me that most of the young men I encountered in the penal system where I was placed had no problem with authority. However, for them, it was the authoritative figure that was always in question. What most of them expressed is that if an authoritative figure had no more to offer them that what they already had, there was no reason for their placement under the authority of that individual. For that reason I tried to offer everything I had and then some every day, to address issues with the mind, body, and soul. This I did for the advancement and growth of another individual. As a result, my team always responded with participation and cooperation beyond my wildest imagination. I'd say that my term as Peer Counselor was a successful time. I truly believe that I had been able to make a difference in somebody's life.

For years, I now believe that I have run from the truth. For years, I have even attempted to deny what was so obvious, settling for a seat in the back of the audience looking on rather than a seat up front in leadership. With everything that I have experienced, learned and witnessed, I now believe that it would be a crime to continue to disregard the gift that is so obviously there. I have finally accepted what I am convinced is true. I have been anointed and equipped with the training and the experience to lead in the Body of Christ. My only remaining question at this point in my life is, 'where will this realization and acceptance take me?'

THROUGH INCARCERATION
GOD DEVELOPED MY CHARACTER

*But we all, with unveiled face beholding as in a mirror the
Glory of the Lord, are changed into the same image from glory to
glory, even as by the Spirit of the Lord. I Corinthians 3:18*

A PRISONER'S MINDFRAME
By Christopher R. Watkins

My institutional life runs short, yet deep and long through my veins.
Years of toil and struggle, months of trial and pain.
Days of hoping and wishing, so tomorrow I shall remain,
The man I have become, and marvel at how far I came.

I looked out through the window at cars and people as they past.
Invisible to those individuals until I am free at last.
Time reminds me of a camera as life goes by in a flash
It records a frozen image that I can look back on and laugh.

If I knew then what I know now, this may have never occurred.
But, I have learned a lot along the way, and
I believe I am being preserved.
So, I could dwell on past events, but, I just prefer
To soak up all of the knowledge I can until my time is served.

$$\text{\tiny{---}\ \normalsize{❖❖❖}\ \text{\tiny{---}}}$$

LIFE LESSONS LEARNED

I. THE AREA OF *LEADERSHIP*

Then the word of the Lord came to me saying, "Before I formed you in the womb, I knew you; and before you came forth out o the womb, I sanctified you, and I ordained you a Prophet to the nations." Jeremiah 1:4, 5 (AKJV)

From the day we are born into this world, we immediately, and, without even realizing it, fall into God's order for His creation. There is a place for everyone and everyone must be in his/her place in order to function to the maximum, God – ordained potential. When I was very young, I always had a problem keeping my toys out of the floor in my room. My mother would come in screaming how the room was a mess and needed to be cleaned. "There is a place for everything and when you finish with it, everything should be in its place", she would say before she threatened to spank me should I have chosen to disobey. Therefore, in the same fashion, I learned to organize things in my life. I learned, as I grew and matured, that authority works the same way. There are never two chiefs of any Native American tribe, nor are there ever two Presidents of the United States of America, at least not in authority at the same time. Scripture confirms this concept - "One Lord, One faith, and one baptism" (Ephesians 4:5 AKJV)!

Why can there never be two? Why does one always rise above the other? Can there be an incident in which more than one are equal in authority and power? In order to answer these questions, I believe that we must go all the way to the top of the 'totem pole' to a point where mom and dad have no say whatsoever – where the Manager, the Principal, or the C.E.O. have no jurisdiction. Our answers lie where Judges and Mayors can only imagine – where Governors and Senators struggle to ascertain – where even the Pastors, Bishops, and Popes must receive guidance. We must seek our answers on that ultimate plane – a spiritual plane – with the One, True and Living God!

I believe it is necessary to begin discussing the concept of 'Leadership' with God for multiple reasons. I believe that the first reason we must begin with God is because leaders are looked upon as the ones who are God's representatives in the church and must set the example for all followers. Leaders in the secular world also are looked upon as those who set the example for how others should govern themselves in many of life situations. People have often attempted to justify their faults or wrong choices by using what a leader has done in his/her life. These people, of course, are seeking an excuse to continue the path they desire to pursue. The Bible describes God as 'Perfect' (Matthew 5:48 AKJV). Even when God "...humbled Himself and manifested Himself as flesh and blood", He remained 'holy and without blemish' (Ephesians 5:27 AKJV). When we examine the example Christ set, it becomes difficult, if not impossible, for a follower of this leadership to find excuse for wrongdoing. He or she may search for excuse, however, they will find none.

> *...leaders are looked upon as God's representatives in the church, and must set example for all followers.*

Why can there never be two, equal leaders? The Bible, teaches that we "cannot serve two masters, for we will love one but hate the other"(Luke 16:13 AKJV). When we think about this, I wonder how many individuals would truly feel that they can bare their all, pledge and maintain allegiance, give their entire lives to two deities and love both at the same level! It's almost like having two jobs, two full-time jobs. It is very difficult to exert the exact same amount of sincere, extreme energy on each job, every day, even if the time issues could be managed. One job will more than likely find the employee slacking, which will not make the boss happy nor make for a good employee record for the future.

Secondly, I believe it is necessary to begin with God because, as you may know, God has no equals. The Bible says, "He is God all by Himself"

(Isaiah 45:22 AKJV). To have an equal would mean that ultimately God would not have supreme authority. I strongly believe that God does have supreme authority in this world, at least in my life. Sometimes leadership borders on dictatorship because when decisions must be made, followers look to leaders to make those decisions. One thing I learned is that everyone is not meant to be in leadership. Not everyone is a leader. The position or office of a leader requires characteristics that not everyone possesses.

When I came to clearly understand leadership, I learned what the cliché', *"He sticks out like a sore thumb"* really meant. Leaders possess certain characteristics that separates them from the rest of the pack, from their followers or team. Giving directives and instructions to others is only a small portion of the duties that most leader have to perform. I believe that a sincere leader at heart will not give any follower a directive or instruction to perform any task that he or she is not willing to perform himself.

One critical character trait that a leader must possess is the right attitude for the job. An individual with anger management issues will more than likely not make a good leader. Also, an individual who is rebellious and not willing to follow leadership above himself, will not make a good leader. A good leader must first know how to follow leadership. I believe that a good leader is one who has confidence that he/she does not have to broadcast – it seems to quietly emanate from the individual.

I'm reminded of the two linebackers in the movie, "Remember the Titans". The story line of this movie takes place in Virginia during the time of racial segregation in the South. Although T. C. Williams High School was one of the first to desegregate, the school left the students to adjust themselves to the new situation of the times. They provided no support to assist the students in navigating these new and unfamiliar waters. The football team was no different. It was a reflection of what the student body was attempting to handle under these new, official racial rules.

As the football camp began, the coach (Denzel Washington), realized that his biggest problem was not who would be the starting quarterback or which plays he should teach the team but rather, how to deal with the mindsets of the team members on the issue of desegregation. The coach realized that the strongholds on the issue of race had to be torn down in the minds of these young people if the team was to be successful. He also understood that he could not accomplish this alone, but, he saw two leaders already emerging from among the members of the team. What the audience had already realized was the fact that the coach had found it necessary to do everything he could to draw every bit of emotion out of these two team members, Gary and Julius. When Gary and Julius finally reached their breaking point, they subconsciously stepped out in front and the rest of the team followed. One of my favorite scenes in the movie happens when Gary confronts Julius following of their grueling three-a-day practices. When Julius told Gary what he thought about the situation, Gary told him that he thought that this was the worst attitude he had ever encountered, Julius responded, "Attitude reflect leadership, Captain." What I believe Julius was trying to say was that in order to become a leader, an individual must have the desire, the drive, and, the enthusiasm as well as natural abilities, in this case speed, in order to be effective and lead a group of individuals.

I have been a member of the African Methodist Episcopal Church (AME) for as long as I can recall. This denomination was established as a legal entity in the year of our Lord 1816, after thirty years of court battles with the White Methodist Denomination. It also took a huge amount of work and courage from the leader, Bishop Richard Allen, who became the first Bishop – the first official leader of this newly formed denomination. Bishop Allen was driven by a desire to worship God in an atmosphere where his people were treated with respect. The final act came on Sunday, November 6, 1787 when the Blacks who worshiped at Saint George Methodist Church in Philadelphia, PA were pulled off of their knees during an altar prayer and not allowed to pray there with the Whites. Bishop Allen and others walked out in protest and Allen, along with others, began to make provision for this fledgling congregation to worship in a place of their choosing. I believe that the fire that was ignited in Allen and others burns brighter and brighter even to this day.

> *A leader must always be willing to take the initiative to do whatever is necessary.*

A leader must always be willing to take the initiative to do whatever is necessary. Perhaps there were other Blacks who were fed up with their treatment at Saint George Methodist Church. There were probably more who were tired of always having to sit in the balcony rather than down on the main floor. However, if Bishop Allen had never taken the initiative to do something about it, I wonder how long would the Blacks have continued to remain confined to the balconies of houses of worship while professing to worship the same God as the Whites. I believe that saying that "You never know how your actions will affect others and the future." Our Creator has a purpose for every one of us in this earth. Pastor Rick Warren, in his book The Purpose Driven Life says believes, "If God did not have a purpose for us, we would not have been born in the first place." I have learned that we are expected to take listen and remain in tune to God and take initiative to make a difference in this world.

Again, not everyone is equipped to become a leader. People in general seem to pursue power and money. Yet, not everyone can handle the privilege and deception of freedom that power and money seem to present. When we examine the statistics of lottery winners concerning their financial situation within five years after the award. Some are deceased. Some behind bars. Then, there are those who lose all of their winnings and then some due to over – spending or over – indulging in addictive vices such as drugs, etc. Uncle Ben told Peter Parker, "With great power comes great responsibility". Others depend on their leaders to make the right decisions. Often the lives of followers are placed in the palm of the leader's hand. One wrong move, a careless or unwise decision of a lead doctor in a heart surgery could possibly prove fatal to the patient.

Humility is a characteristics that I believe a good leader must have. This characteristic allows the leader to have compassion for someone else. I also believe that there are leaders who are not afraid to exercise their leadership, however they are perhaps overly compassionate. They care a little too much. What even the greatest leader must come to accept is that, "We can please some of the people some of the time. We can please all of the people some of the time. However, no matter how hard a leader works, he/she will never be able to please all of the people all of the time". Good followers come a "dime a dozen", but a good leader seems to be more and more difficult to find.

II. THE AREA OF *RESPONSIBILITY*

There is a phrase I have always heard that says, "What's understood, need not be explained." I believe that life would be much easier if this idea was in fact true. In these times of illiteracy and low comprehension skills, that statement does not ring true. In fact, I have recently concluded that not everyone has as firm a grip on reality as I believe that I have. Or perhaps it's the level of maturity that so many young people seem to lack these days. If they were more mature, they would understand the difference between a need and a want. A need is more than likely necessary for survival while a want may be substituted or forgotten altogether. I understand that even though we are obligated and should be responsible enough to make intelligent choices, often times, we still tend to make the wrong decisions for reasons that even we may not understand. This gives me an appropriate entrance into the next topic of discussion.

> *"What is understood, need not be explained. What is necessary should be uncomprising."*

I am convinced that there are people in this world who would rather look good than take care of what is necessary. Michael Jordan could release a brand new, two hundred dollar pair of shoes at twelve o'clock tonight; when the famous athletic shoe retailer Foot Locker opens at eight o'clock in the morning, there will probably be s line outside the store that stretches around the next corner. Some of those there to make the purchase will probably leave with more than one pair. Some may purchase the shoes and everything else including a matching outfit. The sad thing is that these same people may have completely disregarded the electric bill or the phone bill while the refrigerator is also quite bare. In these days and times it appears that too many people find it more important to construct a "front" or a facade than to just simply be who we are and live within our means. I believe that the kind of behavior I have been describing illustrates behavior of individuals that are probably not very responsible or mature. 'Dressing to impress' or to 'Look like money' may be appropriate for job interviews. However, I believe that this way of thinking should never come at the cost of the necessities of life.

These days and times, people in society seem to think that it is more important to construct a front or a facade than to actually allow the public to know who we really are and are not. I have been taught to dress to impress especially when one is interviewing for a job or other important position in life. However, this manner of thinking should never come at the expense of a necessity. I believe that we must learn to take care of the necessities of life first. Some people would rather accept poor health than to spend what is necessary to go to the doctor or purchase the needed medications or other items. Again, I am reminded of the proverb, "What is understood need not to be explained. What is necessary should be uncompromising." Understandably, there are times when certain things in life must be placed on hold. The problem appears to be that some people have a difficult time separating obligations and necessities from desires. Parents should feel obligated to do certain things for their under-aged children without question.

> *Whether we realize it or not, responsibility is waiting around every corner.*

Bills! Bills! Bills! They seem to pop up everywhere all the time. However, I believe that too many individuals have a difficult time distinguishing the bills that are priorities and necessities from others that are not so necessary. It seems to me that a vast number of families have become so accustomed to watching television that all too many people see the cable bill as a priority. We depend on the television and expect it to be there. We forget that entertainment is is a luxury. We must rearrange our priorities. It's important to have the telephone operational so that when the perspective employer calls with information concerning a job, we will be able to receive the message.

Responsibility set within the household; but what about when we step outside of our homes. Whether we realize it or not, responsibility lingers around every corner. Another very important place of responsibility comes in the form of our occupations. To interview for a job is to request trust from that company or organization. To be granted the position implies that one has been deemed trustworthy and have been given the opportunity to live up to it. As soon as we sign the contract or agreement to perform the required tasks for the job means that we have pledged our allegiance to be on time; to complete all assignments; to get along with coworkers; and, to submit to the authority figures as designated.

When it comes to signing contracts and agreements – did we read the fine print. I believe that many people make the mistake of not reading the fine print and then becoming angry when they realize what has been signed. I believe that by not taking the responsibility to read the fine print on contracts and agreements, many people happily sign their lives away. It is our responsibility to to read and seek to comprehend the terminology of the fine print in any document we are expected to sign. We need to understand that we have the responsibility to know the rules of the game we play.

In another area of our lives, most of us know individuals who make promises that they have no intentions of keeping. Some make promises they know that they are not able to keep when they make them. The Bible talks about being "ensnared by the words of your mouth"(Proverbs 6:2). I like to say that people 'offer you a lie' and make it a habit. We sometimes offer God lies whether we realize it or not. Perhaps we were a little too intoxicated one night. "God, I promise", we said. "Please help me to sober up and feel better". "I promise, this is the last time," some

> *Giving them by word was my first mistake because I knew that I didn't really mean it.*

people have said. "God, I promise, if you will get me out of this situation, I will do better." These types of promises are all too familiar. However, we need to understand that we are bound by every lie we tell. I recall the character Wimpy on the cartoon, Popeye. He would always promise to pay for his hamburgers on Tuesday. "I'll gladly pay you on Tuesday", Wimpy would say. When we apply this type of scenario to our own lives, we could ask the question, "Does Tuesday ever come?"

When I was about nineteen years old, my mother and I moved from a rural area in central Georgia to a city in North Georgia. When we moved, I was completing my first year at Valdosta State University in Valdosta, GA. At the African Methodist Episcopal Church, where my mother was assigned as Pastor, I was one of the oldest teenagers in the youth group. Because of this, I was usually the one driving. I remember one particular incident when I neglected my responsibility. I was asked if I could go to the movies with a small group of individuals one night. At the time, however, I had my mind set on some other things. Going to the movies was not a top priority of mine at the time; but, I had promised the other individuals that I would go. Giving them my word was my first mistake because I knew that I didn't really mean it. Needless to say, we all missed the movies that night because of me not keeping my word. I didn't even understand the weight of the situation and my responsibility in it until the mother of one of the individuals involved took the time and patience to explain it to me. I felt terrible knowing that I had neglected friends, especially when I had not intended for things to happen the way they had. The Bible tells us that we are to "let our 'no' be 'no' and our 'yes' be 'yes' (James 5:12).

Making commitments take many forms, from a situation as sacred a marriage, to not upholding a friendly agreement. Even a situation where a bar-b-cue is planned and each individual has promised to bring items to make the festivities come together. No item is any more important than the other when they are all needed to make the event a success. Not only is every individual responsible to bring the item promised, but it is an agreement that should be upheld.

> *We should always remember that there are two or three sides to every story.*

Responsibility also plays a major role in discrepancies we find in our lives, no matter how major or minor we believe them. I believe that men many times have trouble communicating with one another. It is my opinion that mane often allow their egos blow situations out of proportion. Communication is so very important that I believe that if men could discuss a perceived problem, we might not have half as many misunderstandings and complications that sometimes result from microscopic matters. I believe that if we are too big for ears, why have them? Cut them off since they seem to be useless if we are not willing to listen to one another. I have always been told that we have two ears and one mouth so that we can listen twice as much as we speak.

Whenever there are discrepancies between individuals, we should always remember that there are two or more sides to every story. Two or more people equals a conflict that sometimes can be sparked by no more than a few words from someone completely outside the situation. I believe that we cannot even fathom how many people are dead today as a direct result of gossip, hearsay, or, words that are totally unfounded. Bad news, or bad information, spreads like wildfire on a wind. However, good news seems to never surface or never remain surfaced for any significant period of time. I have learned that it is irresponsible to speak about or spread words about something I know nothing of. I also believe that even if we have full knowledge if a problem or situation; unless the individuals involved request from us a possible solution, we continue to be an outsider. I have grown to believe that this should mean that our services should not be offered, even if we believe them to be needed.

I have never been much of a ballroom type dancer. I don't know how to waltz. I have no experience in performing the fox trot or the salsa. However, the one thing I do believe is that, as the cliché says, 'it takes two to tango'. Obviously, we are not literally discussing dancing, but, the concept remains the same. Just as in the dance with two individuals, both parties play a part in the action. During the course of a particular dance performance, one partner will move in one direction while the other partner cooperates by completing their particular part of the dance. Neither can stand still while the other dances if they want the performance to exemplify excellence. The same concept holds true when there is a conflicts. When I was a child, my older sister and I would get into knock-down-drag out brawls. No matter how much either of us would try to declare our innocence, my mother would always point out the fact that both of us were guilty of something. Each of us had played a part in the conflict. I believe that we must always remember to examine ourselves when we are at odds with someone else. What we may have done could have been coincidental or unintentional; but, some way somehow we have contributed to the conflict by omission or 'co-mission' – what we omitted or what we have 'committed'.

> *However, I have learned in my spiritual journey that there are no accidents or coincidences in the Master's plan.*

I entered the sixth grade in school in the fall 1996. I attended the newly built Middle School in Augusta, Georgia. I remember that we had a security officer at the school whose name was Michael Stephenson. As I recall, Officer Stephenson was a very nice individual. Unfortunately, Officer Stephenson died the following summer in an extremely sad situation. However, in my spiritual journey, I have learned that as sad as his death was to so many, there are no accidents or coincidences in the 'Master's' Plan. Believing this as truth, I will now use Officer Stephenson as an example in this next subject.

I have learned that sometimes giving someone the 'benefit of the doubt' can surely be deadly. When we have a responsibility to carry out a procedure, I believe that it is our job to eliminate the the benefit all doubt. During the summer of 1997, while on duty, Officer Stephenson came in contact with a young man he knew. Whether he was going to arrest this young man or not is not certain. What we do know is that in the midst of his confrontation with this young man, there must have been the implication that Officer Stephenson would have to arrest this young man. The problem is that Officer Stephenson placed this young man in his car but never followed through and handcuffed him. Since he knew this young man, Officer Stephenson gave him the 'benefit of doubt' that he would do anything to harm him or to try to get away and avoid arrest. However, this

> *...a lapse or failure of one individual has the potential to make everyone look bad.*

young man pulled out a gun and shot and killed Officer Stephenson and left him dead in the street. It is believed that Officer Stephenson had thought of this young man as a friend which is why he considered the handcuffs unnecessary. I would determine that this idea called giving the 'benefit of doubt' blinded Officer Stephenson to the reality of the situation and to his responsibilities in his job. Sadly, it cost him his life.

After sitting in my mother's congregations Sunday after Sunday; during Revivals; Church Anniversaries; and, other celebrations, I came to realize that there were some phrases that appeared frequently in the sermons that were given. It didn't matter if it was my mother, one of the preachers on staff, or a guest preacher, I often heard the promise that if we died in Christ or as a Christian, we would hear God say to us, "Well done thou good and faithful servant. You have been faithful over a few things; come on up now and I will make you ruler over many things" (Matthew 25:21). I have asked 'Why are the few things so important?' 'What is about the things that are small in number and appear so irrelevant that God considers so important?' Most people don't even understand how the smallest detail can be so hugely critical.

I once had a guy tell me that he always did a little test, so to speak, with the women that he would take out on a date. He would always open their door, as a gentleman should. The test came in whether or not the young lady would reach over and open his door. He felt that if his door remained locked, it was an indication of a selfish character in the young woman. This young woman would not last long with him because of his unwillingness to deal with the selfishness in her character. This same concept could hold true in little children. I believe that at least in the Black community, we teach little children to say 'Thank You'; 'Yes ma'am'; 'Yes sir'; because we know that some people they may meet will interpret actions, gestures, and statements in different and sometimes twisted ways. The expression 'Thank You' simply says that we appreciate something that has been said or done for us. It doesn't matter if it was a kind word, a smile; or, something that we may have brushed off as minuscule, microscopic, or unimportant. The expression 'Thank You' simply shows appreciation to the person who had said or done something.

> *A good word attached to one's name means everything!*

We discussed responsibility in employment earlier, however, I want to return to that briefly to make another point. In one's workplace, an individual worker is not obligated to another worker unless assigned that way. Employees are not required to take on another employee's duties unless instructed to do so. However, when more than one person is needed to accomplish the same task, a lapse or failure of one individual has the potential to make everyone look bad. When I was incarcerated at a State Prison in South Georgia and trying to acquire a job detail in the gym, I wound up becoming a medical orderly in the clinic. While I didn't want the position in the clinic, I accepted it for reasons irrelevant to this point and will not be discussed at this time. What I will say is that I have become the type of person who wants any task where my name is attached to be completed in excellence and come out sparkling. Therefore, while I was there, I always worked for excellence and was able to maintain my position in the clinic longer than the average inmate.

In spite of my desire for excellence, I was assisted by a couple of coworkers who couldn't care less about working and doing a good job. We were responsible for the cleaning and sanitation of the medical ward.

However, the staff members always saw me working but they always saw my two coworkers slacking on the job. A good word attached to one's name means everything. A good reputation can be a tremendous help in getting one's 'foot in the door' in places that may otherwise be difficult to access. It's important to cross the threshold of certain places in life the right way rather than trying to break in the wrong way.

Everyone does not do janitorial work, however, I feel that this occupation is what will best fit my next argument. The guys I worked with at the facility in South Georgia just could not seem to grasp the concept of initiative. It's obvious to me that if something needs to be done, and we are an employee, we should do it! We should not rely on the next person that comes around because that next person just may be the supervisor who will evaluate us negatively. The next person might also be the one to do what needs to be done and in so doing the job may attract the right person who will grant them access into the right door.

Taking initiative...or to complete a task with a spirit of excellence hekos one to learn and grow.

I was the same way as those guys I had worked with when I was growing up. I did not like to take the time to do a good job at just about anything my mother told me to do. I couldn't understand why, when my mother would ask me to do something like clean the kitchen, she would come back after I had completed washing the dishes and ask me if I had wiped down this or wiped down that, or empty this. "But you didn't tell me to do all of that!" I would argue. "Why should I have to do all of that?" I would ask. She would always answer that we should learn to take the initiative to do some things that we were not specifically asked to do as a part of completing the whole job. She would always explain and outline tasks that were included in cleaning the kitchen and end with the statement, "Cleaning the kitchen is more than simply washing the dishes." With this she was teaching me to look at the whole job and to take the initiative to complete the whole job with a spirit of excellence.

I learned that this situation involves as mental maturity that some, unfortunately, may never grow to understand. 'Why is it so important?', some may ask. I believe that it is for the same reason that football players and their coaches prepare all year for certain games; for the same reason millionaires expand their companies in an effort to make more money. Taking initiative to do more than one may have been asked to complete or to complete a task with a spirit of excellence helps one to learn and grow. I believe that's why football player, Peyton Manning knows what defense a team will execute before the ball is snapped. He spends hours upon hours in the film room, studying and analyzing footage of opposing football teams. I believe that Tyler Perry is so wealthy because he didn't just write a few screenplays. He acted as well and now has ventured into cable television. He reached for excellence in whatever he did and is now wealthy beyond his dreams.

Before I was incarcerated, talk about taking responsibility in one's life and striving for excellence in every task was what I would have called gibberish, if there is such a word. I even recall getting locked out of my own house on my birthday because I wasn't responsible enough o keep up with my own key. One of my high school football coaches told me once that my mother did too much for me. I couldn't understand it at the time. However, as I reflect back in his statement, I realize that he was probably exactly right. This particular coach, 'Coach Anderson', always had an aggressive way of dealing with me and I will be forever grateful to him. I didn't have my father or many father figures in my life at all, but he was one of them. I don't believe that there is a way anyone can go into and endure a traumatic situation like becoming incarcerated and come out the exact same way they went into it. I perceive things from a totally different perspective now since my incarceration. Part of the difference is that I now understand how critically important it is to maintain a responsible character. It's unfortunate, but I believe that there are a lot of other people who will have to learn these lessons the same way as I did – the hard way!

> *I believe...I was exposed to the characteristic of humility in the form of animation.*

III. THE AREAS OF *HUMILITY* & *LOYALITY*

I believe that this character trait is a precious jewel, a priceless, valuable heirloom that has been missing from the jewelry boxes of many, so-called "Cleopatra's" for generations. It has become like a long, lost Leonardo Di

Vinci masterpiece; or, a lost pair of sandals worn by Christ, Himself. Here I would like to discuss what I believe is a long lost character art of epic proportions that could be as detrimental to one's health as oxygen. Very simply put 'Let's talk about Humility'!

Humility is the exclusion of one's self, specifically for the benefit of someone else. Perhaps this is why dogs are considered 'man's best friend' and not parrots or rabbits or any other domesticated animal. Dogs have been known to develop such an attachment or relationship with a master that to observe the two in interaction one could assume that the dog can actually read the owner's mind. I believe that there is something very moving about the way some dogs are protective of their masters. It seems that at a moment's notice some K-9 companions would willingly lay down their lives for their masters. I have seen doges that seemed to sense the mood or disposition of their caretakers and could change their depression with what looked like a single touch. Obviously there are cartoonists that believed the same as I.

I believe that in my generation, I was exposed to the characteristic of humility in the form of animation. As a youth I loved a cartoon character named 'Droopy Dog'. If one has ever had the pleasure of watching a Droopy Dog cartoon, then understanding where this is going is easy. In one particular episode, Droopy Dog and his co-star were mining for gold. They had a 50/50 agreement for splitting everything they mined until, ironically Droopy struck gold. After that, the co-star made every attempt to erase Droopy from the picture. All Droopy wanted was his 50/50 share, never more. The greed of the co-star was the very thing that finally caught up with him and 'did him in'. Droopy humbly, yet unknowingly offered to his co-star what they both thought was a bag of gold. However, the co-star dashed off with a bag filled with dynamite – the same bag of dynamite he had tried to give to Droopy to wipe him out! I watched Droopy all the way through high school until another humble K-9 caught my attention. Cartoon Network developed a new line of cartoons that included one of my favorites called 'Courage the Cowardly Dog'.

In the story line, Courage had been abandoned as a puppy, but, was found by a lady named Muriel who lived in the middle of nowhere with her husband, Hustus. There were always weird, creepy and possibly dangerous things would repeatedly arise which would call for Courage to live up to his name and protect the couple who had rescued him. Courage had obviously formed that bond we previously mentioned between the dog and his master because he could be relaxing with Muriel all day. All of a sudden, his contentment in relaxation would be interrupted when some weird and dangerous incident would take place. At the drop of a dime, Courage would be up and doing whatever necessary to protect Muriel and Hustus. Sometimes, believe it or not, Courage would use his computer reference, which he kept in the attic of the house, to diagnose the problem and receive a recommendation as to how to resolve it. Regardless of the diagnosis, by the end if the story, Courage is right back where he desires to be, relaxing with his masters – most of the time.

Of course, there are those individuals who might prefer something a bit more realistic than animation. Well, please allow me the pleasure of directing your attention to one of the humblest characters one could ever watch on the big screen. Allow me to present what I would call 'the pride and joy of Alabama' – a war hero, an All American college football star; and, a millionaire. His character name is Forest Gump. Forest Gump appears to be mildly mentally handicapped, however, I believe that he understand much more than he is given credit in the story line of the film. Forest

> *As we gro older ans begin to matue into adulthood, I believe that sometimes it can become difficult to maintain a humble nature.*

believed the scripture 'God works in mysterious ways' (Isaiah 45:15); and, according to his understanding and belief, Jenny was moved out of her father's house to him. Contrary to Jenny's belief, Forest understood love and recognized his affection for her. Forest understood destiny, as Lieutenant Dan Taylor saw it, and began a quest of his own. Finally, I believe, Forest understood very well what it meant to be a true friend. We could ask Lt. Dan how much he, in the final analysis, appreciated Forest pulling him out of the forest in Vietnam. I believe his friendship meant a lot to Bubba prior to his death during a battle of the war. Last but not least, his love for Jenny caused him to rescue her many, many times from potentially dangerous situations.

In my personal opinion, Forest Gump wasn't the least bit as slow as his character appeared to be. Whatever he did or whatever his intentions may have been, he was always sincere. He sincerely loved Jenny with all of his heart and wherever he was, she stayed on his mind. That's the reason several of her potential boyfriends kept getting beat up. When Forest thought there was a problem or that Jenny was in a difficult situation, without question or hesitation, he was there to the rescue. I wonder how many men would be willing to remain and fight for the honor of a woman he has been waiting for in the rain for hours, only to find her in the car and the arms of another man.

Forest sincerely loved his friend Bubba and immediately saw beyond what others saw as a negative condition – Bubba's big gums – and recognized the man on the inside. With all of the people Forest pulled out of the war zone, he acted with the intentions of rescuing his friend. The scene at the river when Forest made a statement concerning Bubba was one of the most touching in the entire film. Forest said to himself, "Bubba was my best, good friend and even I know that ain't something you can just find around the corner." I love Forest, because for me, everything he did came from the heart, a humble, loyal heart. His humble nature ultimately gave him everything in life he desired. And, as Forest would say, "That's all I have to say about that!"

> *Experience is also a very valuable teacher!*

As we grow older and begin to mature into adulthood, I believe that it can sometimes become difficult to maintain a humble nature. I believe that different situations in life can require one to have a commanding attitude. I don't believe that this has to alter one's personality, however, it may become difficult sometimes to break free from the role or to switch attitudes in different situations. I believe that when an actor receives a part for a character in an upcoming movie, many times they may take that character home with them. I believe that without realizing it, they may literally become that character. Without realizing it, one may actually lose oneself to the character one if playing at the time.

Another situation that may give rise to this situation might be when an individual is given a position of authority. People in positions of authority make decisions sometimes on an hourly basis concerning everything from employment to termination to supplies, etc. I believe there is a role that must be played in this situation in order for the employees to respect and honor the authority of the one in charge. Sometimes, individuals become what I would call, 'Power Struck' and unable to handle the position and be fair to the employees. They forget that they were once in the same position as those who are now their subordinates. I believe that some people lose their compassion for others when they become elevated to higher positions. They appear to lose their humility and sense of loyalty. It's ironic that compassion and loyalty may have been the very character traits that made them eligible for the position of authority in the first place. However, somewhere, somehow, it became lost.

I believe that every stage that one reaches in life has the potential to bring one more and more clarity and insight concerning certain situations. It is important to remember, however, that each individual is different. Each person's perception is his or her reality. Experience is also a very valuable teacher. One individual who has never been in management would more than likely view a management situation differently from an individual who has been in management for several years. If a person has never experienced a situation, it is difficult for me to believe that this individual could instruct me as to how to handle this same type of situation. One thing I believe that helps in handling a situation which may be a potential problem is to step back and dissect each part to determine what is truly the problem.

> *...people respond differently to a confident individual...*

In maintaining one's sense of humility and dealing with other individuals, I believe it is important to try to discern what type of person the other individual truly is and not who he/she appears. This, I believe would assist us in avoiding arguments with some individuals, because we could determine that the argument really is not necessary. Case in point – when my incarceration time was almost over, I found myself frequently in the presence of a certain individual. We would always seem to 'bump heads' around the topics of sports television. We would argue for fun about almost any topic that surfaced. In the process of arguing with this individual, it became apparent to me that he was not as knowledgeable as the other guys in the place with us, yet, he would continue to make himself available for debate. There were times when he would initiate the debate with some absurd comment. I soon began to dismiss this individual as ignorant of the topics we were discussing, however, his comments would often irritate me to the point of responding. I had to constantly remind myself of who it was that I was dealing with in an effort to maintain my sanity and humility.

On the other hand, there happened to be another guy in the same area who was very knowledgeable on the topics of our discussions. This gentleman was very intelligent, very coherent, and very aware, however, he, at times, could not accept the fact that some of the conclusions he would draw in the conversation had holes in his rationale. He would often try to cover his holes with more information but the holes kept surfacing every time. I began to observe how irritated he would become through the change in his voice and in his demeanor. Rather than add fuel to what appear to me a possible fire, my humility would allow me to allow him to be content with his assumed correct comments. This, I believe, is sometimes necessary in keeping the peace. A humble individual would be able to move forward from a situation of this nature. I believe that some things must be allowed to pass one by in order to avoid being run over by a proverbial train or eaten by the proverbial lion when it comes to debating and maintaining humility.

Because I believe humility is extremely important in everyday interactions with others, I also believe that having confidence in oneself is also important. I believe that people respond differently to a confident individual than to one who appears to have no confidence. I recall the Holiday Inn Express commercials in which the simple vacationer or other traveler appeared to be a doctor or classroom genius all because having slept at the Holiday Inn Express had given them the confidence. The people were shocked to find out the real identity of these individuals because they had demonstrated overwhelming confidence. Being a young man, I have frequented the social scene enough to have seen that women appear to love confidence in a man perhaps more than some of the other characteristics that some guys would have us believe. However, I believe caution should be the operative word here. There is always another view to the spectrum. Too much of anything can become detrimental for an individual's well-being, and, having too much confidence is no exception. I believe that a confident man knows what is best for himself and the people around him and works to make those conditions a reality. On the other end, a cocky, self-absorbed, self-centered man is usually not concerned about what is best for anyone but himself. The confident, humble man knows when the task at hand is too much to bear alone and has no problem seeking help from others. The cocky, self-centered man may realize that the task is too great for himself alone, however, his pride causes him to make excuses rather than admit he needs anyone else to assist him.

In the book "Forty-Eight Laws of Power", the author makes the statement that one should not outshine the master. However, I was taught that the student is expected to become greater than the teacher. However, in dealing with the self-absorbed, self-centered individual, I believe it may be more peaceful to allow that individual, at times, to believe that he/she is the teacher or the master and move forward. I believe that it may be better to stroke an ego sometimes than to become an ego. Why allow someone to make your life difficult when it is not necessary and doesn't have to be that way. One of the main abilities we have that separates humans from other animals in creation is our ability to problem solve. Some primates have the ability to use items as tools without having been taught; and, a plethora of animals communicate with each other. But human beings are unique in that we have the ability to take a complex problem and dissect it with precision in order to determine the best solution to the problem. I believe that when we find ourselves in situations with individuals such as those with very little humility who would seek to steal our peace and joy, we should put that problem solving skill to work.

While I was still incarcerated, I received a detail or job in the medical ward of the institution. I was probably the youngest inmate to have been given a detail in that area. I don't know if my age was a factor but I seemed to always have been the focal point of scrutiny. I was harassed repeatedly and on one occasion, fired for no reason. I remained humble and silent as my superiors rambled on about things that either were irrelevant or absolutely had not happened. To the surprise of some, I found myself reinstated a few days after the incident. I believe that my spirit of humility demonstrated the very kind of character that has the power to move an individual forward in life. I would advise anyone to hold fast to a humble character no matter what for I continue to believe that humility is a lost diamond that for me is now **DISCOVERED**!

IV. <u>THE AREA OF RESPECT</u>

It has always fascinated me that several individuals can take the exact same action, for the exact same reason or purpose; and, interpret everything in as many different ways as there are individuals. Let's begin with something as fundamental and simple as fire. Fire may be the most important discovery for mankind for a myriad of reasons. I don't believe that we can honestly say that civilization would be what it is now without fire. Yet, we know that it demands a certain amount of respect because of its potential. Fire can wither be devastatingly destructive in the wrong hands; and, at the same time, fires can also be extremely helpful handled correctly, with the right amount of respect from the right hands.

Passion is often symbolized by fire which means that we are also discussing the emotional as well as the physical. One phrase that I have heard frequently is "Having fire in one's eyes" which depicts extreme anger or aggression. Fire is also one of the factors that determine whether or not our cars will start when we turn the key in the ignition or press the appropriate button. At a young age, we learn how to handle electrical outlets and hot stoves in our homes in an effort to prevent house fires. On a camping trip, individuals must be careful to find a clear, clean place to set up so that dry leaves and trees will not become ablaze. I believe this little thing called an ego, when mishandled, can become as destructive as electricity.

> *I understand now more than ever that respect is a two way street.*

When we discuss the topic of respect, I am reminded of how as a child I was taught to say "Yes ma'am", "No ma'am", "Yes sir"; and, "No sir". I believe that most children, when I grew up, were taught these niceties or manners, as we were told, before they are even potty trained. I will never forget one day when I was talking with my little niece and I heard her say "Yes sir" to me. Since I am still a young man in my twenties, I quickly dismissed this notion as unnecessary for her to respond to me in that manner. However, I quickly realized that my little niece was growing up under the discipline of the same woman who had taught me the same things. I felt that I was disrespecting my mother to tell my niece that this was not necessary. In a sense, I would be erasing her teaching rather than respecting it and teaching my niece to respect my mother's teachings.

What about a spouse? How do we demonstrate respect for the one we say that we love the most? Some may think it unnecessary to deal with respect when it comes to the spouse. However, ask the wife how she would feel if the husbands stops wearing his ring without a legitimate reason. Ask the husband how he feels about the so-called platonic relationship with her ex-boyfriend. And obviously each of these scenarios could easily be reversed. I believe that without communication each of these situations could be disrespectful behavior that would definitely warrant the question "Why?". Each of these situations could also very easily be avoided by respecting the spouse enough to communicate. Because I am a man, I understand that a man wants to know who is around the woman he loves. I have always heard that the idea that 'communication rules the nation' is an accepted philosophy worldwide. I often regret some things concerning my high school days. I recall taking a Spanish course because, initially, I wanted to become a translator. However, being young and ignorant to some facts about life, I believe that I prevented my reaching that aspiration. My Spanish teacher and I kept clashing in our interactions. I now believe that perhaps it was because she saw potential in me that I could not see in myself. Perhaps it was because I was being difficult in response to the difficulty I thought I perceived in her towards me. Whatever the case, I now feel that I lost out on an opportunity to fully break a language barrier.

I understand now more than ever that respect is a two way street. We must respect decisions that other people make concerning their lives and we must respect their decisions as well. From another side of the matter, however, we must respect suggestions from people whom we care about and who care about us, especially when they are trying to help us. We may not want to heed ultimatums from others, but we can, none the less, listen and consider their suggestions. We must realize that everyone needs help sometimes on this road called life and burned bridges are never good if we want to continue this road.

I've quickly come to learn that when we treat others with disrespect, it changes their perspective concerning you and the kind of person you are. Hopefully we would not go to someone's home and purposely trash it. Likewise, we would not make a pass at or disrespect someone's significant other. These actions would not only change a person's perspective of us, but, often times the results are that violent and aggressive actions take place. I believe that there have been many deaths as a result of someone not showing respect for someone else. I don't believe a little common courtesy would hurt anyone.

Professionalism, I believe, is a form of respect that I believe is critical when one represents a multi-million dollar corporation, an institution, or, an organization. Persons in these positions must really carry themselves well in the eyes of the public. In the world of professional athletics, courtesy and respect are still critical to success, I believe. The world was glued to the television during the 2014 NFL Playoffs, watching the as the game between the Seattle Seahawks and the San Francisco 49'ers come to a climatic ending. However, we all became transfixed to the drama that ensued from Richard Sherman and Michael Crabtree. Even though many individuals may have felt that Sherman was not the most likable person, I believe that it was still poor sportsmanship, poor professionalism, and disrespect for Crabtree to put his hands in the man's face in the manner in which he did. Good sportsmanship – win or lose – is always a plus for anyone. At the level of 'professional' athlete, I believe many people expect better.

This incident was not the first time Sherman had made such a spectacle of himself. During the previous year, following their wild card game against the Redskins in Washington, Sherman had a memorable run in with an offensive lineman from the Redskins' team.

Sherman - "You need to get out of my face little man!"
The Offensive Lineman - "Or what?"
Sherman - "Or I'm gonna punch you in your s***!"
The Lineman - "Do it!"
BANG!!!

I'm sure many football fans remember that incident! Of course, I don't believe that Mr. Sherman is a misfit, a villain, a thug, etc. I don't believe he would have been able to maintain the GPA that he had a Stanford University had he fit any of those negative labels previously mentioned. I believe he could, however, work on his people skills and his professional courtesy. There is no questions that he is presently one of, of not the best in the game of football. But, I believe it was probably difficult dealing with the loss of the game that his team had lost, especially to a team like the Seattle Sea hawks who seem to have players like Sherman at every position.

Now I'd like to discuss what I would like to call the "Rabbit Hole" of disrespect. Let's chase this rabbit like Alice in Wonderland, down the rabbit-hole and pretend we are 'late for this very important date'. I don't believe we will lose this rabbit because disrespect of one another, I believe, is sometimes an extremely large part of what may be wrong as we deal with one another. I'm also positive in my belief that what we will find if we were to examine disrespect is an abundance of ignorance. It is always a possibility that the seemingly disrespectful individual is ignorant of the fact that he/she has been disrespectful. I've seen situations where an individual who feels he/she has been disrespectful confronts the other individual and the scene turns bloody. I believe that men have a lower tolerance for disrespect than women. Also, I believe that women have a tendency to stop and think more than men do. They don't appear to act on impulse like most men I have observed. When we do this, we will realize that all disrespectful acts are not intentional and once we stop and think about the situation rationally, we will begin to see that.

> *...men seem to have a lower tolerance for disrespect than women.*

So, what do I believe we should do, as a result of my experience, when we feel we have been 'slapped'? What is the next step we should take in resolving the confrontation? Some individuals take the road of aggression, forcing their will, physically upon another. It just seems to me that some individuals find it easier to just hit someone in the mouth while in a fit of rage. However, the aftermath of having taken this path to resolve conflict will more than likely result in much more anger. However, I believe that there is always a second option, and, with just a split second of thought, one could find it and created peace in the situation. The question then becomes, 'can we repair friendship after so much chaos?' 'Can we actually reconstruct relationships?' I believe it is absolutely possible because I don't believe in the 'one and done' scenarios. As of right now I know things about certain people, things they have done that I believed they shouldn't have done, especially since it involved them attacking another person that I thought they considered a friend. Sometimes, I believe, God allows certain situations to be placed in our paths in order to see how we will react or respond to it. I truly believe that God blesses us when we forgive other. After all, He had to forgive us.

While I was still in high school, I had a friend that I truly considered a brother. Should he ever read this, he will know exactly who I am referring to and the situation that occurred. One Summer I got a job at one of the local grocery stores in the town where we lived, partly because he was already working there and recommended me to the manager. After work, my walk home usually took me by his girlfriend's house. One day, as I was on my way home, she happened to be sitting outside of her house on the steps. When she saw me, she called me over. I was not prepared for the news she was about to share with me. She shared with me that her boyfriend, my supposedly brother, had approached my girlfriend in an intimate fashion. I didn't know how to respond to this news. I couldn't believe that he would do this, especially since his girlfriend was so attractive; and, he and I were supposedly so close. I asked her a few irrelevant questions until two very important questions finally came up. The first one was "What had my girlfriend not told me about this since I had spoken with her since the incident?" and secondly why had 'she' told me this. I stood there for a few minutes until I realized what was actually happening here. I realized that this young lady, my friend's girlfriend, was figuratively leaving the door open for revenge against my friend, her boyfriend.

> *...when we open up a can of worms, they immediately try to get away from us.*

So what was my next step? I felt that I had to make a quick decision that would ultimately affect me for the rest of my life. I thought about revenge because I was angry. But, I did not want to create a cycle that I felt would continue, and, I really did not want to lose my friend, especially since nothing further had happened between my girlfriend and him. I eventually thanked her for the information and left. I believe we should always remember, when we open up a can of worms they immediately try to get away from you. The idea of revenge can consume an individual. I don't believe that we should allow someone or something to control us that way. Some time it's best just to let it go. He's still my partner, my brother.

We even call each other's mother, 'Mamma'. I believe that the past is the past and that's where we should leave it, behind us. I did learn from the situation, however. I never put anything past anyone anymore. The one we least expect could be the very one to disrespect us. I also believe that a little love can go a long way!

V. A *HIGHER POWER* – FOR ME IT IS CLEARLY *GOD*!

Because I am the son of a pastor, for a large portion of my life, I have been in church. It has been instilled in me for as long as I can remember to always trust and place my faith in God. Until this very day, I can tell you that I am a firm believer in Almighty God. I believe, and have seen with my own eyes, that anything you ask, believing, God will do. It took me years to actually open my eyes and realize what was transpiring, not only in my life, but also throughout humanity.

In the African Methodist Episcopal church, every Sunday morning, we recite "The Apostles' Creed", which reads as follows:

> I believe in God the Father Almighty, Maker of Heaven
> and Earth; and in Jesus Christ
> His only Son, our Lord, Who was conceived by the holy
> Spirit, born of a virgin Mary,
> suffered under Pontius Pilate, was crucified, died and was
> buried. On the third day He
> arose from the dead, He ascended into heaven, and sits on
> the right Hand of God, the
> Father Almighty: from thence He shall come to judge the
> living and the dead. I believe
> in the Holy Spirit, the Church Universal, the communion
> of saints, the forgiveness of
> sins, the resurrection of the body, and life everlasting.
> Amen

The life, death, and resurrection of Jesus Christ is the foundation for everything Christians hold true. Muslims do not hold this as truth. They do not believe that Jesus Christ was indeed who he proclaimed to be. Muslims believed that Jesus was a mortal man and a teacher named

Isa, but, not the Messiah. What is interesting to me is that Muslims have been so against Christianity for years and yet the religions are strikingly similar. For example, the Muslim's Torah actually is the Christian's Old Testament. Not only that, but also, I have learned that Islam, Judaism, and Christianity all trace their roots back to the same person, Abraham. I truly believe that one of these days they may be able to come to common ground since they really do have so many similar beliefs. They are also all centered around One, Omnipresent, Omnipotent, Omniscient Figure. I believe you can call him whatever name you desire, he is still God.

According to what I have been taught and what I have witnessed in my life, He Is the Great 'I AM'. He is the 'Alpha and the Omega', the 'Beginning and the End'. He is All knowing, and, All powerful. He is Majestic and Mysterious. Who else can take credit for the construction of an entire universe in just six days? Abraham Lincoln once stated, "I can see how it might be possible for a man to look down upon the earth and be an atheist. But, I cannot conceive of how he could look up into the heavens and say there is no God." In Mark Cahill's publication, "One Heartbeat Away", the author took a very traditional approach to describing God's Power. Mark Cahill very cunningly examined the feud between science and religion.

> *He IS the Great I AM. He IS the Alpha and the Omega!*

I found Mark Cahill to be a very intelligent individual who is able to paint visual images on a level I can only dream to reach one day. However, I will attempt a description of what I believe illustrates God's power, in my own words. We all probably know that birds fly south for the Winter. They naturally have an in-born sense of the changes in the seasons and automatically take that journey to warmer climates every year. There are some species of water creatures who automatically migrate back to the place where they were born when it's time for them to mate or to lay their eggs. Why do these animals migrate in this fashion? How do they know when it's time to go? How do they know how far to go? How do animals such as bears know exactly when it's time to hibernate and what to do in order to prepare for hibernation? There are fish in the deepest, darkest parts of the ocean that don't have eyes! Every creation is evidence of a creator and human beings are no different.

In the book of Job, we find God reminding His servant of Who He is. God questioned Job in chapter 38:4 with these words, "Where were you when I laid the foundation of the earth? Who determined its measurements? Surely you know! Or who stretched the line upon it? To what were its foundations fastened? Or, who laid its cornerstone when the morning stars sang together and all the sons of God shouted for joy?" In the seventeenth verse God asked, "Have the gates of death been revealed to you? Or, have you seen the doors of the shadow of death? Have you comprehended the breath of the earth? Tell me, if you know all this." Then, like the Master Craftsman God is, He pointed out to Job the differences in creatures of the same kind. Job 39:13, God states "The wings of the ostrich wave proudly. But, are her wings and pinions like those of the kindly stork?" As awesome as all of these are, there are still creatures being discovered and classified even to the present day.

I believe that scientists have somewhat piqued our curiosity when they crossbred a lion with a tiger and call them 'ligers'. They are huge creatures! The problem is that these creatures can never be released into the wild since they would be foreign to just about any ecosystem on earth. They will live out their lives in captivity being trained, fed and handled every day. I believe that this once again illustrates and reveals God's Sovereignty. Everything in nature exists in a delicate balance. Every creature has a place and a purpose. God shows us that while His work is often imitated, it is never duplicated!

> *...once agin this illustrates and reveals God's Sovereignty!*

What is it that separates us from God? If we were created in His image, shouldn't we be able to reflect the characteristics of our creator? Sure! But we can never entirely be like God. His very thought processes go beyond anything we could ever fathom. The Word of God says in Isaish 55:8, "for My thoughts are not your thoughts, nor or your ways My ways...", says the Lord. He further stated, in 55:9, "...for as high as the heavens are above the earth, so are My ways higher than your ways and My thoughts higher than your thoughts." Most of us, I believe, would not even know what to do with or how to use such superior knowledge as that which God possesses. God is Wisdom and Knowledge. I would have trouble with a simple math problem. I know I would not be successful trying to divide X and Y chromosomes, forming an individual's gender, or creating oxygen. The audacity of human beings to even imagine that we could sustain an energy such as the sun for even one day.

I want to show you what I believe true power looks like. Picture a snowflake falling to the earth in a snowstorm. You catch one in your hand and examine it closely. You immediately notice the intricate pattern in its design. Once it dissolves in your hand, you catch another one and closely examine this one. Again, you notice the intricate detail in the design of this snowflake. However, what you realize is that this design is significantly different from the first. As you continue this examination of individual snowflakes, you realize that each one possess its own unique design. In the larger picture of God's creation, you realize that each human being is just like each snowflake. We each have been created with our own unique design, yet, we are all still created in the image and likeness of God. Now that's power. What a Mighty God we serve!

Guidepost has a publication entitled, "Angels on Earth" which I truly enjoy reading. In my opinion, the stories in each publication illustrate the power of the Almighty God like none I have ever read. The stories that these believers tell always blow me off my feet. I used to wonder why I have never had the opportunity to actually see a heavenly being for myself because I have always wanted to encounter and angel in my life. Finally, the epiphany hit me one day that I didn't need to actually experience an angel in order to get me to believe or to strengthen my faith. I realized that these stories were about people who actually had the need to come face to face with one of God's messengers, or, were in desperate need of that experience. Because God is omniscient, all knowing, He knows exactly what is needed in our lives and what is sufficient for every situation. I've never had the need to experience a heavenly being to cause me to believe that God is Who God says that He is.

I once met a young man while I was incarcerated who told me the details of an experience he'd had. He said that he was on drugs and had no money to buy more in order to satisfy his habit. On this particular night, he said that he sat in the parking lot of a Walmart store preparing to commit armed robbery on an unsuspecting, innocent individual in order to get more money for drugs. He said that all of a sudden, a lady appeared outside his car window, on the driver's side where he was sitting.

Not knowing where she had come from or exactly what she may have wanted, he proceeded to roll his window down so that he could speak with her. When he did, he received something he had not expected, words of comfort for his situation. According to this young man, the woman said to him, "Son, It's gonna be okay. Go on home. Tomorrow you will probably get some money. Look for it." After she turned and walked away, he thought about her words and reluctantly went home. To his surprise, the next day he received a huge check that he wasn't expecting in the mail. Now, you tell me, what transpired here? I'm not sure what anyone else would call it but I would qualify it as a miracle! I believe that this young man had just come in contact with an angel and didn't even realize it until years later. God's power is absolutely amazing to me! Every time someone sets out to prove the Bile nothing but fictional stories, the only thing they end up finding is truth!

What is sleep? I wonder if anyone can accurately define this unconscious state where our minds and bodies are still active.

> *He received something he had not expected, words of comfort for his situation!*

How are we able to awaken from sleep and not die or go into a coma? How is it that the moon is controlling the tides on earth, and, that changes in the moon appear to affect our and even cause changes in our bodies? And, even though the moon controls so much on earth, without the sun, there could be no life here on earth. We cannot answer these questions because we do not have the proper knowledge. I even learned that our eyes actually capture images upside down and our brains actually interpret them as they are! Once we realize that we don't have all of the answers to life's puzzling questions, we begin to wonder who truly does. I know I do. I remember the days when I would ask my mother a million questions. Sometimes I really wanted an answer and sometimes I was just curious to see if she really knew the answer. Most of the time she could answer my questions, but there were those time when I would receive an aggravated, "Chris, I don't know."

I don't believe that we will ever receive all of the answers we seek in this realm of existence. I don't believe that we even have a firm enough grip on what life truly is. I believe that there is so much out there, in life, waiting to be discovered that we will probably never be able to realize it all. That's the reality of this life – here today, gone tomorrow. We live for a time, grow old and then we return to our creator. Psalms 102:26, 27 state,

> "They will perish, but You will endure; yes, they will all grow old like a garment, like a cloak,
> you will change them and they will be changed. But, You are the same and your years will
> have no end." Psalm 102:26, 27

The sad thing is that these days, we don't have to be old to die. But Christ is eternal, immortal; immune to sickness, disease, and death. But, even Christ put on a mortal body and became like us as He walked among us. What do we think that Christ experienced back then that we don't experience right now? There is nothing new under the sun. God already knows what we are going through. Everything is in His time and for His purpose.

I don't believe that there are ever coincidences in God's creation!

One reason that I believe it is so difficult to understand the scriptures is because of the difference in the times and cultures. If someone of Jesus' day would attempt to describe an airplane to us today, we would probably break out in laughter. The people of Jesus' day only had their cultural items to reference. It would be the same if we attempted to describe or understand things from Jesus' day. And, if we were to encounter futuristic technology, we would only have the cultural items of this day to reference. In the book of John 3:4, Jesus was speaking to a ruler of the Jews named Nicodemus. Jesus was attempting to explain to Nicodemus the one and only way to enter into the Kingdom of God. The problem arose because the spiritual metaphors that Jesus used to describe this path sailed completely over Nicodemus' head. Likewise, we too have a difficult time explaining the things of the spiritual realm simply because we have not seen that realm. Nicodemus asked, "How can a man be born again when he is old? Can he enter a second time into his mother's womb and be born?" When Jesus spoke of being born again, the only reference point Nicodemus had was the human flesh, from his mother.

I believe that this conversation with Nicodemus was not coincidental. I don't believe that there are ever coincidences in God's creation. I don't believe that anything happens unless it is ordained by God. Sometimes when people die young, there are many who will say that they died before their time. I don;t believe that anyone leaves this world without an order from the Almighty God. I have a friend by the name of Jerry Carter who can witness to this belief. When I was in high school, Jerry begged a young man to give him a ride home one day after school. The young man refused to give Jerry a ride, but, when this young man turned out onto the road from school, her was hit by a SUV and died right there in front of the school. Yes, Jerry was saddened by the death of a school mate. However, at the same time, he was glad that he had not been in that car because the wreck was so horrific that Jerry would probably have been killed as well. I believe that it was not meant for Jerry to be in that car. I believe that God is in control.

...the word coincidence has to be a man-made concept because nothing God does is by coincidence!

For the basketball fans, let's think about Derek Rose. I called it a coincidence when he tore his ACL one year in the playoffs. Rose had made the exact same move a hundred times or more and had never torn his ligaments. But why did the coach keep him in the game with a twelve point lead and time winding down in the fourth quarter? I believe that, like many things in our lives, it was meant to happen. Also, I believe that it was meant for Miami to win all that year because Chicago was a serious threat in the East that entire season. I believe that the word 'coincidence' has to be a man-made creation because nothing God does happens by chance or coincidence.

I can remember when the Olympics came to Atlanta, GA in 1996. My mother took me to see one of the baseball games. Our seats were high under the second deck which made it rather difficult for me to catch a foul ball. However, late in the game, as people began to leave and sets became available, I asked if we could move down a little. My mother wasn't budging but she told me that I could go down closer because our seats were also in the shade of the third deck. I didn't move down either, but the very next batter hit a foul ball into the exact seat I had been looking at to move down and occupy. That may sound like a coincidence, but, I don't believe so. If I had moved to that seat when my mother said that I could, I not only would have had a chance to get that first ball, but also, two or three more that were hit into the same general area. To me, that was more like a missed opportunity because I believe that the Holy Spirit had tried to prompt me to move. God knew that I had come to the game hoping to have the opportunity to catch a ball and I believe He tried to give me one but I failed to accept the opportunity to receive it. I believe we all could witness those types of situations in our lives when we look back and realize how we failed to get in position to receive what God has for us.

It appears to me that the way we live today, there are so many non-believers. It seems that there are so many thieves, murderers, sexual deviants, etc. that just about every law God handed down to Moses, thousands of years ago, is broken in some way, shape, form, or fashion not just every day, but so many times a day. It seems we have very little trust for one another. It seems we have very little respect for one another. And, it seems there is absolutely no love for one another, unless, in the case of a blood relative. Then, I believe that in all too many families, even blood relatives are outcasts for little or no understandable reason. In the Bible, 1 John 4:20 reads as follows: "If someone says he loves God, and hates his brother, he is a liar. For he who does not love his brother whom he has seen, how can he love God whom he has never seen?" A very valid question, indeed. It seems to me that we have adopted hatred as an everyday way of life and have accepted it as being the 'way of the world'.

I believe, however, that the truth is that we have all dealt with hatred or dislike on some level. Since my incarceration in 2004, I have dealt with this myself on numerous occasions. In one case, it was with my father. My father has never been a positive influence in my life. I probably have not even seen him in over fifteen years and he still lives today. I remember becoming very angry with him one day when I was visiting him and I felt he neglected me by leaving me with his daughter, my half-sister, whom I had never seen before. He had been informed that we were coming but he left before we arrived. I could not understand why he would not have wanted to bring his two children together if for no other reason but for us to get to know one another. Over time my anger grew to the point where I wanted no dealings with him period.

Coming into the prison system gave me a pretty good insight into this situation. I have met guys with multiple kids in different parts of the country. From all that I could determine from my interaction with these men, they loved their children but for whatever the reason, they could not be with them. Whether it was a disagreement between them and the child's mother or a legal issue, they seemed to have legitimate reasons for not being able to be there. I came to understand that life doesn't always place one in position to be available when we want. I realized that I really didn't know what the circumstances were that caused my father to do what he did. Over time, my wounds healed and my anger subsided. I can never change the fact of who my father is but I could never imagine my life any differently. I have committed that if I were able to speak with him, I would want him to know that I love him even though I have not seen him in years. I would also love to see my sister that I was with that day again.

My other situations of anger deal with some of the people whom I have met while in the prison system. I feel that I have come in contact with some individuals who, for whatever reason, have some of the ugliest, nastiest, filthiest attitudes I have ever seen. Many of them try to down play their attitudes by saying as an excuse, "It's just a job." However, I for one cannot accept that as a reason for their attitudes. I cannot accept the fact that one individual can treat another individual in such an ugly fashion and be content with it. Not every officer in the Georgia Department of Corrections is as I have described. This says to me, that the others who are choose to act this way. It literally took me years to learn to deal with people with these kinds of attitudes. Then, I was blessed enough to make it to a placement in a Transitional Center during my final year of incarceration. It was there that I came to the realization that I cannot escape individuals like this no matter where I would go. I believe that this made it easier to deal with the individuals with the ugly attitudes because I now knew what to expect. I believe, however, that these are people that we must pray for as we keep moving forward in life. We cannot allow the poison of their attitudes to keep us from advancing in whatever our endeavors.

> *...these are people that we must pray for and keep moving forward in life.*

I believe that people who can treat others in ugly ways, as I have witnessed, reveals that the individuals who are able to do this must be mentally and emotionally afraid and feel that they have to intimidate in order to have control of the situation. I don't believe that an individual like this could explain the definition of love if they were living around it and experiencing it firsthand. A Bible passage in 1 Corinthians 13:4 states, "Love suffers long and is kind. Love does not envy. Love does not parade itself and is not puffed up; does not behave rudely; does not seek its own, is not provoked; thinks no evil; does not rejoice in iniquity, but rejoices in the truth; bears all things, believes all things, hopes all things, endures all things." This, I believe, is the definition of love in a nutshell.

I believe that when an individual loves another, they only want to see the best in that individual, and for that individual. I believe that, as the scripture says, love is not selfish, and, love does not have cruel intentions. I also believe that there are some people who cannot see past themselves, but, this could ultimately bring harm in the long run. I have also heard different philosophies concerning love. One individual that I met split love into two parts in his definition. He believed that an individual could either have love for another or be in love with the other. While I can definitely see how he could come to that thinking, I believe that I agree more with others I have heard define love. I met one young man who stated it very simply by saying that once an individual honestly fell in love with another, nothing else would matter. This, I believe, is what 'unconditional love' looks like. Another young man I met stated in a discussion on defining love, that if two individuals come in contact with, get together with each other, and, they are willing to treat one another the way they each want to be treated, by all means they should hold on to each other.

I don't believe this young man realized that he had understood a fundamental concept better than most people. It appears to me that the theory is that the word love is a verb, an action word which indicates that something is done if there is truly love. I'm sure we are all familiar with the immortal words of Jesus in John 3:16 of the Bible. Jesus said, "For God so loved the world that he gave his only begotten Son..." Most people who define love as action will agree that two of the most important words in that passage are 'GAVE' and 'BELIEVES". God gave. Christ gave. We must believe. It's the same as when a parent gives a child a new toy and the child says 'Thank you. I love you.' Both of these are signs of love one to another. I believe that words, by themselves, are empty especially when not backed up with action.

So where does this leave us when it's all said and done? When we have closed our tired eyes for the final time and taken our final breath of life; when only our actions can speak for us and we can repent no more, where will our destination be? Here we find Jesus making a promise to those who earnestly and sincerely believe. There's the word 'believe' again. In John 14:1, Jesus begins by saying, "Let not your heart be troubled; you believe in God, also believe in Me. In My Father's house are many mansions. If it were not so, I would have told you. I go to prepare a place for you, and if I go and prepare a place for you, I will come again and receive you to Myself so that where I am, there you may be also," That must be love, in my humble opinion. In this day and time, I believe that we all have to be careful who we bring home with us, because we may never know an individual's intentions. But, for me, God has made it crystal clear that His intentions are for us to dwell, or live, with Him for eternity. I believe His actions have already spoken for themselves.

So where is heaven? How do we reach heaven? What is it like there? Jesus said in John 14:6, "I am the Way, the Truth and the Life. No one comes to the Father except by me." What I believe Jesus is saying that we need to believe and live our lives accordingly. I don't believe this is any different from the concept of taking certain actions to go on vacation. We'll never get to our destination without getting in a car, or other means of transportation. However, whether that car is a Buick, Camry or Lexus, it will never be able to touch the streets of gold. I believe that this place called heaven is a physical place prepared for only those who possess a 'humble and contrite heart'.

The Bible tells us that sickness and death will cease to exist. It describes a paradise only for the righteous, courageous souls who have fought the 'good fight' and are rewarded with everlasting life. However, I believe that our getting to heaven is directly related to the decisions that we make down here. I believe that disrespecting the next person simply because that person happens to be there, is not acceptable for admission into the place we call heaven. As I mentioned previously concerning the employees of the Department of Corrections, I have encountered many different people with different attitudes. Some choose to treat other individuals as human beings while some choose to treat other individuals with nasty, rude attitudes. However, I believe, it is always their choice as to how they treat others. Hebrews 13:2 states, "Do not forget to entertain strangers, for by doing so, some have entertained angels and did not know it." In my opinion, no one should ever intentionally mistreat another human being or handle them harshly because, as the scripture states, that person my not be who he/she appears. This is one of my favorite scriptures in the entire Bible and the following verse hits home also by saying, "Remember the prisoners as if chained with them, those who are mistreated since you yourselves are in the body also." I wonder how many people have no idea that this scripture exists.

On May 13, 2014, I made a choice to leave the transitional center in a very disruptive manner. I allowed my self-control to slip and I became very irate and confrontational with the officers on duty, which ultimately got me the ticket I wanted, out of there. While I wanted nothing more than to leave that center, looking back, I would pick a better way to do it. However, that's the choice I made and I will have to forever live with it. Each of us should ask ourselves the question 'What would I do?, Which road am I walking? Which path am I taking? I realize that none of us are perfect and we will make mistakes from time to time. However, I believe that even when we stumble on this road called life, if we have the faith we can be picked up and guided onward. Have you ever wondered why God does not fix all of the potholes in our path on the roads of life. I believe that's an excellent question. I also believe that God is also asking why we don't pay more attention to the signs He places on our paths along the way. If Peter had kept his eyes on Jesus when he walked on the water, in Matthew 14:22 – 32, he would never have sank into the water. I remember when I first learned to drive, I would always hear, "Watch where you are going. Pay attention to what you are doing." I believe that the same advice is relevant on this journey toward heaven that we are traveling. I believe that there is too much going on in life to take our eyes off of God.

How much more can I say about a man who split the Red Sea and fed a multitude of 5,000 men, not to mention women and children, with two fish and five loaves of bread? Not only that but everyone was filled and there were twelve baskets full left over. What can I say about a man who changed water into wine and re-attached a man's ear back to his head. I have to say, I have seen God work in my life on numerous occasions, even though I don't always so what I am supposed to do when I'm supposed to do it. But believe me, I know what God is capable of doing if we only believe. We all need something or someone to believe in and I choose to believe in Jesus Christ.

VI. <u>THE AREA OF COURAGE</u>

In the late eighties to the early nineties, there emerged a series of movies on what I felt was an extremely popular animated television show that informed everyone who to call "When there is something strange in the neighborhood." The theme song was so catchy and had such a courageous edge to it that it is still sung to this day. The title of the song was "Ghost Busters"! I especially liked the bridge portion of the theme song which emphatically proclaimed, "I ain't afraid of no ghost!" In the movies, the Ghost Busters were the popular heroes of the physical realm because they were the ones who would fight against and rid the city of any spiritual invaders, such as ghosts.   I believe that one thing this song and its movies did was to instill in kids that they don't have to be afraid of anything. They can stand up to anything that came their way physical or not.

I believe this was somewhat the same thing as the movies about Superman, Wonder Woman, and, my own personal favorite, Batman. When we consider the story of Batman, although fictional, Bruce Wayne, the man who played the part of Batman, must have been a compassionate and courageous human being to lay down the wealth and riches that he possessed in order to defend a city whose citizens considered him was a vigilante. Yet, whenever his city was threatened, Bruce Wayne dressed at a moment's notice and volunteered his services to Gotham City. He even took years to train and conquer his own fears in order to become the man that he was. This, I believe, is an example of a true hero.

I believe that there is a process involved in having the courageous acts that are needed and it begins with a thought. A thought is the foundation by which everything materializes. If I wanted to build a mall, a school, or an office, without the first idea, nothing will ultimately take shape and become a reality. That's why I have always believed that all sports are ninety percent mental and ten percent physical. A player has to visualize the game before the game is played. This will lead to the next step in this process that I mentioned.

The word, or spoken word, I believe, is the next step in this process. I believe that the spoken word is used as a tool to enlist the mind and imagination of other individuals. Most of the time, one person will not be able to build a structure by himself/ herself. Here's where deeds take over. When all of the necessary individuals are engaged with their minds, imaginations and their bodies, it is possible to make that thing that began as a thought a reality. At this point, there could be 150 workers, gathered, working together, to bring this structure into reality. What began as a single, solitary thought from one individual, now has enlisted all of these individuals to complete it. What does this have to do with being courageous? I think just about anything and everything. It took courage for the individual with the first thought to step out on their own and begin to enlist the necessary others to assist with this project. We tend to fear the unknown or anything that is outside of what we consider our comfort zones. Just being alone for many people is a frightening place to be. If an individual fails to step out, and enlist someone else, dreams or ideas could be destroyed simply because of the fear of the unknown.

I believe that it takes a courageous person to be able to stand alone regardless of criticism and the seemingly ever present ridicule of outsiders. The fact of the matter is that not everyone is going to accept any one way of thinking on anything. It seems to me that some people will find any and every way to kill the movement of your theory, if given the opportunity. I believe that we must be brave enough to stand and look our adversary in the face and tell him that we have no fear of anything. It take a brave person indeed, to stare down the barrel of a gun, knowing that the trigger could be pulled at any moment. These could be examples of consequences of standing alone, in my opinion.

It seems to me that things don't always go as planned and as expected when we are standing alone. Let's not glorify being alone because standing alone, sometimes means going against established protocol, against established laws and tradidions. What happens when an unstoppable force meets an immovable object? What happens when a courageous man, or woman, becomes firmly planted in his/her beliefs which causes him/her to have to stand against the powers that be. I remember the day I chose to leave the Albany Transitional Center. I had become fed up, as the cartoon character Popeye would say, "That's all I can stand and I can't stands no more." What angered me even more was that the problems and concerns I was upset about had not originated with me. When I first arrived at this center, the residents were telling me the exact same things I was seeing until the day that I left, but nothing was ever done to correct the problems. Even though I knew the Center was where I needed to be; I knew the Center was the help I needed before being released, I just could not deal anymore with what was happening there. In spite of the fact that people may say that I was crazy, I needed to leave and knew that I would be content with that outcome. Now, being honest with myself, I feel that there was probably a better way to handle the situation. However, I only regret my actions to a certain degree and I had no problem accepting the consequences.

The awesome thing about that entire incident was the reactions that I received from onlookers. I've been told that whenever something has been place on and individual's heart to do or say, there must be follow through with the action. Why? I believe that it's because one never knows how his/her actions can affect someone else. My actions that day could have been the defining factor in someone else decision making. Watching me that day, could have set the standard for someone else's next move. I believe that sometimes, standing alone can inspire others who are onlookers. I believe that sometimes watching someone else have the courage to take action could instantly give another the strength to step forward. I don't believe that I was the only man there who felt the way that I did about the situation. However, I was the only one who stepped out against it. My hope was that someone else would stand up and take action against their treatment. My sincere hope was for a domino-effect of individuals taking action against the unfair treatment. When one falls and manages to touch another, the energy generated is almost impossible to stop.

When more people join the action, more often than not, there are different minds coming together for the same purpose. Because there are different minds in the process, I believe, there could be different ideas about how to handle the same issue. The Civil Rights Movement in the 1950's and 1960's is a prime example of what I am talking about here. During the movement, some people marched, some boycotted, some staged protests, but they were all taking action for the same purpose. And today, I believe that we all see how far African Americans have come in this country, even though we know that we have a long way to go. However, I believe that as long as the problem persists, the action against it should never stop. I believe that no matter what kind of opposition we encounter, there is always a way to deal with it.

I believe that courage sometimes takes some people by surprise and shocks others as they stare at the actions taking place. For example, I've seen a fight break out in the middle of a room and others in the room watch intently unless the brawl starts rumbling their way. In this case, I have seen the onlookers just move and continue to watch. However, I believe that if a parent was frantically trying to move an automobile off of a child, anyone who rides or walks by would stop and help in the situation. I have also seen an individual's actions bring opposition from onlookers. We must understand that everyone may not be in agreement with our actions. However, I believe that a truly courageous person is his/ her own person and doesn't need others to validate decisions made or actions taken. I believe that truly courageous individuals have no fear. Ms. Rosa Parks wasn't afraid of going to jail that day when she refused to give up her seat on that bus. Ms. Parks was tired after having worked all day and she didn't need an instigator to convince her to keep her seat. Because of that demonstration of bravery and courage, she is known as the mother of the Civil Rights Movement. It is ironic that she started a "Movement" by "NOT moving".

VII. T x 3 – TYING THINGS TOGETHER

In the preceding pages, I believe I have given just about everything I have learned over the past few years during my incarceration experience. In approximately six chapters, I have attempted to bare my soul concerning my life and my experiences. I believe it would be almost impossible that no one could relate to any of it. I believe that in the confines of these pages is a lesson for everyone in every walk of life. Since I have now spoken about these topics, I will go in depth and attempt to illustrate to you why

I believe that I have been able to acquire these character traits through the experiences of my life.

LEADERSHIP

I believe that this is the easiest character trait to discuss. Since I was a child, my mother has often said to me many times that she believed that I had been called to the preaching ministry. Until this day, I still do not believe that this is my calling. However, what I will say is that I do believe that I have been trained to lead, perhaps not a congregation. Since I was very young, I have many time been given the opportunity to be behind a microphone, in front of a crowd. I have also often been called upon from a group to speak or perform for various purposes.

The first time I was approached about playing quarterback on my football team, it was the farthest thing from my mind because of my small size. It was during my seventh grade year of Middle School, right after baseball season that my coach informed me one day that he was searching for someone to play the position of quarterback. As long as I had been playing football, I had found that I had a strong arm and ability to throw a football well. However, in spite of the fact that I was able to throw a great distance, I had never envisioned myself throwing "snaps" as a quarterback. When I was younger and had played in the recreation football league, I was always the "Center". My coach knew that I had good grades and that I was an intelligent football player.

My coach also knew that I was not necessarily going to be alone. There were two other guys on the team, that I recall, who were also looked upon as leaders, therefore, I would not have to worry about having too much pressure in the game. I remember looking out over the team one day as we were preparing for a game and thinking, "This is my team". We looked like a band of brothers who were ready for battle. I believe we rode that energy all the way to the winning trophy. I recall the game we had played against one of our biggest rivals, Seago Middle School. Our coach had warned us that we would be in for a tough game and that we should not underestimate this team. And, at halftime during the game, we found ourselves down by a significant amount in the score. But, somehow, some way, our locker room talk bonded us together and we were able to come from behind to win thirty-six to twenty-two. I'll always remember that game because it taught me that when leaders mess up, team members don't allow him to forget it. I threw what to be my only pick of the season into that game. The next day, in class, I was met with an "interception man" sign. Kids can be cruel.

Now the football field was one thing, but, the church was something altogether different. Since, of course, my mother was the Pastor, I was always volunteered for events that I normally would have declined. I remember one year when I was chosen to perform a fragment of the Dr. Martin Luther King, Jr. speech, "I Have A Dream". Because I wanted my group to look good, I gave the recitation my best effort. We "tore up" the sanctuary. In other words, people were on their feet yelling and applauding like crazy. Easter speeches, Nativity Scenes, I was a part of them all. This always seemed to place me under bright lights and behind a microphone.

When I was in the eighth grade, I was given an assignment to write a speech titled, "Optimism in My Life". The winner at the classroom level would automatically be placed into the competition at the city-wide level. I truly had no intentions of winning at all. However, before I knew it, there I was, competing at the city-wide level. Until this day, there are still those who believe that I should have been the city-wide winner. There were those who said that the winning student ventured off the assigned topic much too often. At the end of the day, I received a resounding applause for my efforts and many who commented how I had done a good job. I now believe that it was basically all practice for what God has in store for me.

When I was incarcerated, I would never have thought that those leadership skills and public speaking abilities would ever be put to use. I was wrong. I believe I have done more public speaking and have been in charge of more operations as an incarcerated individual than I ever would have been on the streets. I have taught Bible Study classes. I have been in charge of a group of individuals within a program; and, have been asked to direct a skit, which was scheduled for performance during Christmas in 2013. However, due to circumstances beyond our control, it was destroyed in one fatal swoop. Had we been able to present this skit, it would have been highly entertaining.

I believe that leaders are always the ones out on the front lines fighting for the people behind them. When something goes wrong, nobody likes to take the blame. However, the leader usually gets the blame, simply because he or she is in charge most of the time. However, there is one thing that I have learned about a good leader is that a good leader is one I believe can take the criticism and keep on going. A good leader is also compassionate and always has his/her team members' best interest at heart. I believe that I am that kind of leader. After a life of trying to avoid the truth, once again, it is staring me directly in the face.

RESPONSIBILITY

I believe that when a child grows up and begins to venture out on his/her own, one of the most important characteristics parents evaluate in an effort to determine the amount of freedom to allow that child is the sense of Responsibility and how they handle themselves. This is probably the defining factor for parents to determine the maturity level of their children. I believe that most parents would be far more reluctant to allow significant amounts of freedom to a child who has not demonstrated a reasonable amount of responsibility. I believe that the story of the Prodigal Son in the Luke 15 is one of the best examples of a child who has not acquired a reasonable amount of responsibility but was given the maximum amount of freedom to choose his own way. This young man in the bible story lost everything because of his lack of responsibility with all the blessings he had been given from his father. When I left home and enrolled at Valdosta State University in Valdosta, GA, I gained a real taste of what it means to be responsible for one's self, not on jut one occasion, but also on many occasions.

I remember being awakened by my cell phone ringing one morning and because I was not expecting a call from anyone, I almost let it ring without answering it. However, something made me answer, and the lady on the other end of the line was from the cell phone company informing me that I had a past due payment and wanted know how I was going to take care of it. I had just gotten paid from my job at the restaurant on campus, but, it was not an awful lot of money. I had just enough money in the bank account to pay the cell phone bill, but I was left with almost nothing until the next pay check. However, I did have a functioning cell phone and felt good that I had paid the bill myself.

On another occasion, I really got a taste of responsibility when the battery died in my truck, unexpectedly. Once again, I had just received my pay check from my job and was on my way to the store to buy a few things that I needed, including gas. When I completed my purchases and tried to crank the truck to return to my dorm, it wouldn't crank. Right next door to the store, however, was an auto shop. The diagnosis, a completely dead battery. The cost to replace it was eighty-three dollars, which was just about all of the remaining amount of my almost one hundred – twenty dollar weekly, part time pay, and I still needed to do my laundry. Since it was the weekend, I also needed to buy some food in addition to doing the laundry. My mother would always say, "Money sure doesn't go far." These incidents were about to cause me to believe that she knew what she was talking about.

When I was about sixteen years old, I recall getting a job one summer at a local supermarket which was part of a chain. I really just wanted some pocket-money for the summer, at this time. One of my best friends, who was also working at this store, played a major part in helping me to get hired at this store. However, I learned very quickly that the real trick would be in keeping the job once hired. I never imagined that I would have situations test me like these at a grocery store. Boy, was I wrong! When I arrived at work one day, the weather was already quite cloudy. Within an hour, it seems that the bottom fell out of the sky with rain and hail, thunder and lightning; and, strong winds. Guess whose job it was to gather the carts from outside in the rain? First of all, lightning and I do not get along at all. I tried to wait until the downpour had eased up, however, I believe God must have been in the mood to laugh. As soon as I ran out to get the carts, the bottom fell out once again! It seemed that every time I had to run out and gather carts that day, there were more and more carts and harder and harder rain. In addition to that, the lightning actually struck a car in the parking lot as soon as I had run back inside. I was scared to death and wetter than a used beach towel.

I believe that even though I was a responsible individual, I was still unjustly fired from this grocery store and accused of acts that looked like irresponsibility. At 7:00 PM, each evening that I worked, my job was to pull the produce from the shelves, turn the water off and turn off the lights in the dairy department. Then I was to clean the bathrooms for the evening. For whatever reason, at 7:00 every evening, there was one female supervisor who would inevitably call me to the front of the store. Each time she called me away from my duties caused me to require more time to complete those duties, and she would repeatedly call me away. Without warning I was fired because she felt I took too much time completing those assigned duties that she repeatedly called me away from. Sadly, this was not the last time I would be tested with an unjust firing from a job.

When I was incarcerated in South GA, I believe that I was unjustly fired from my job at the medical unit of the prison. The other inmates in my unit and I had been preparing for a Christmas program which I had been given the responsibility of directing. I had asked the ladies in the medical unit to save some boxes they were emptying so that we could decorate them and use them as presents in our skit. On the weekend before the skit was to be presented, I gathered all of the boxes, put them in a bag to take them to be decorated or wrapped for the skit. On the way back to my dorm one of the officers stopped me and accused me of stealing the boxes and concealing contraband in them. He never once checked the boxes, but eventually destroyed them looking to see what was in them. The skit was ruined, and, because I was fired, we would not be able to present the skit. I felt terrible that I would not be able to do this because I love Christmas. Now that the skit had been canceled, I also had to answer to the woman who had trusted me enough to assign me the task of directing this program. She was disappointed but she realized that it was beyond my control.

HUMILITY

I believe that this may be the most important characteristic that I learned during my entire time in the prison system. I honestly believe that no one likes the boastful, proud, obnoxious individual who always has something to say and always wants to be the center of attention. On more than one occasion, I have witnessed an individual with those character traits becoming the focal point of much anger and aggression. I also believe that I have seen this more in the prison system than in society in general.

I believe that humility will not permit an individual to do or say things they have no intentions of admitting or standing up for. I recall that prior to my incarceration, I worked with young man by the name of Cliff. We both were majoring in Mass Media at the University; however, he ended up hosting a show on one of the local radio stations and invited another friend and me to be on the broadcast with him one day. On one of his Saturday broadcasts, I believe that Cliff overstepped his bounds and insulted a host from one of the other shows at the radio station. I personally didn't remember what my friend Cliff had said, but the other host remembered every word. That same day, the other host made it his mission to shoot back at what he perceived was his attacker. Well, I believe this is how "mess" sometimes gets started. A friend of Cliff's heard what the other host had said, came and reported it to Cliff and wanted to know what he was going to do about it. In the words of the friend who reported the statement, the guy had 'called Cliff and his show out', which was an insult.

I was surprised because I honestly could not recall anything that Cliff had said of a derogatory nature against the other radio host. Because I consider myself a man, and had been a participant in the radio show in question, I felt that we should rise to the occasion and offer necessary apologies. When I told this to Cliff, he had every excuse one could find why we should not stand up and attempt to reconcile this situation. We literally had to drag Cliff down to the radio station so that we could put an end to whatever this was that had gotten started.

I remember a guy that I met while I was in prison and I felt that he had the "biggest head" (meaning that he was extremely puffed up with pride and a self – centered attitude) that God had ever allowed any one individual. He was forever bragging about the things he could do, the things he had; or, the women he'd slept with, making statements such as, "On the streets I had this." And, "On the streets I had that." "On the streets I had her and her." But, one thing I came to discern about being incarcerated is that an individual in prison, could be anyone and anything he/she wanted to be, as long as no one else knew the truth. This man must have been everything but an astronaut, so he said. However, none of us had known him when he was, 'on the streets'. I almost said "Captain of a Ship", but, I had also met one of those as well. And again, none of the others of us had known him prior to his incarceration. However, I also learned that, in prison, just like on the streets, when one keep people wondering with the fabulous tales, sooner or later 'inquiring minds' will want to know the truth. The introduction of cell phones into the prison system soon made finding out the truth possible. Someone looked the self -centered gentleman up and even called someone that they knew from his hometown. Hardly anything this man had spoken about turned about to be the truth. Once it became known that je was a liar, life was not as fascinating for him as it had been. There were those who intentionally made his life less comfortable from that moment forward.

I do believe, however, that it was so difficult to be humble while incarcerated. My experience was that there were so many different personalities in such close quarters on a daily basis, with all of their different mood swings and attitudes that I found it difficult to treat everyone equally and with respect. I finally decided that the best way to keep down confusion and to keep myself away from problems was to eliminate myself from the equation. My motto became, "Keep your composure, keep your cool, and above all, keep your distance". I continued to remind myself almost every day of one final point, "Don't allow outside influences (Those people and situations outside of yourself) to impact and/or reflect upon you, as much as humanly possible."

RESPECT

In my opinion, respect is a two – way street. I believe we must give respect in order to receive respect. I also believe that I have always tried to give respect to others, in spite of the fact that some individuals make it extremely difficult. There are so many individuals that I met in the prison system who demand respect but are not willing to demonstrate respect for others. I have even thought that perhaps some of these individuals have had a severe mental problem. I could never understand why any individual would expect others to bend over backwards for them when they were not willing to so the same for others.

The culture of institutional life in the correction system in rough, to say the least. It appeared that every man wanted to be the 'baddest' man on the block, the 'king of the hill', and would run over whoever necessary in an effort to get there. As I observed all of this, I realized that those individuals who always wanted to vie for the top didn't understand that they became a target for everyone below. And, needless to say, some of the individuals below didn't waste any time aiming at the bull's eye, especially if there had been a past altercation between the two of them. That was simply fuel for the fire. One thing I observed, was that the men in all three of the different prisons where I was placed during my incarceration definitely did not respect a person who looked down upon them with a condescending attitude. I believe it's because everyone has the right to a certain amount of respect, regardless of who they may be.

I learned that once an individual, even in incarceration, is in a particular place for a while, people would begin to notice how that individual carries and conducts himself. I believe that an individual who didn't spend a lot of his time in the midst of trouble gained respect and recognition. I believe that is ultimately how I made it safely during the ten years of my incarceration. I was never the one who was always loud and into arguments with the officers and police. I stayed to myself and didn't harm anyone (who didn't deserve it). I always tried to conduct myself as I believed a man should. I took that attitude and behavior with me every time I was moved and was fine wherever I laid my head. I learned that others are much more willing to come to your aid when they know you are not the one who started the commotion. Why? I believe it's all because they respect you.

I was the youngest child in my family and had never had the opportunity to play the role of 'big brother'. Yet, when I came to prison, I found myself in the midst of guys younger than myself who respected me enough to hear what I had to say. So what did I do? I took every opportunity I could to play the 'big brother'. I know of at least one guy who paid attention to the thing I was telling him and the advice I tried to give him. When he left I could even see evidence that some of what I had said had penetrated his thick skull. This young man showed signs of improvement until the day he left. He took care of himself better. He calmed down a little. When he left, he sent me a positive message from the other side of the compound. I was touched to find that something I had said or done had made a difference in someone else life. That experience caused me to realize that there were some guys who were actually looking for guidance.

One of the things I believe that I observed was that many of the inmates disliked some of the people in authority because they carry themselves in such a disrespectful manner. It appeared that their whole persona said "I don't care about you", and they seemed to display it even in the manner in which they walked as well as in their actions. I don't believe many people want to work for or with an individual they feel is not concerned about them at all. Ironically, there are some people who have to work in this kind of situation, but, I don't believe that it has to be this way.

A HIGHER POWER

To speak about the Maker and Creator of the heavens and earth is as necessary as it gets. There is so much that I could say about the God that I serve, that I don't even know where to begin. I believe that I have seen God do something awesome in my life every day of my life. Furthermore, just as that song I have often heard sung in church says, "He may not come when you want Him, but He will be there right on time." I don't believe God has ever been off schedule in my life as He has blessed and provided for me. He is the number one reason that I am able to write and share these thoughts and lessons I have learned during my incarceration experience.

I believe that one thing God has really done in my life is to teach me how to pay attention and to pray. When I was younger, there was a period when I dreamed about snakes every night, and I didn't know what the dreams meant. When I was in the Cobb County Jail, I met a man who had the gift of being able to interpret dreams and he told me that the snakes were symbolic of demons. I felt that the demons oppressing me was the reason I was in so much trouble when I was a younger person. And, now that I was older, I still didn't know what to do to combat or fight against the demonic oppression. Remembering some things I had heard my mother say, every time I went to sleep and dreamed about snakes, I would wake up and rebuke them in the name of Jesus. Once I began doing this, I believe that my life became a lot easier. As a matter of fact, I don't believe that I have ever been in a situation where I have prayed, and, God didn't work that situation out in some shape, form or fashion.

I believe that I have seen God move people out of my life. I believe that God has moved me out of the oath of trouble on multiple occasions. I prayed that God would move me from the Albany Transitional Center, and within two days I was moved from that center. I believe that God has given me a certain gift of discernment concerning people that I have come in contact with. On several occasions, it has proven to be right on point. I believe that as the song says, "I can see clearly now, the rain is gone. I can see all obstacles in my way." God has promised us a bright sun shinny day if we would ever put our trust totally in Him. I believe that even though I am not where I need to be yet, I am getting better every day.

<u>COURAGE</u>

When we speak of 'courage', I think of the Disney movie, "The Lion King". Mufasa told Simba that "Being brave doesn't mean you go looking for trouble." I could not agree more. Being courageous is all about having the heart of a lion when it's necessary. I believe that when courage is necessary all too many people run scared. I believe that too much fear of anything can cripple an entire nation of fighting men. But I also believe that all it would take is for one soldier to stand up and face the enemy with no fear. We need to remember what the Apostle Paul told Timothy, his spiritual son in one of his letters to him. Paul said, "God had not given us a spirit of fear, but of love, power and a sound mind." (2Timothy 1:7)

I believe that this is the same reason that parents teach their children to stand up to bullies. To allow an individual to continue to intimidate demonstrates submission to that individual. I don't believe that we should submit to anyone except God and the authority He places over us. God has given us the strength to overcome any and all obstacles that the enemy may place in our lives. What fear should we have if God is with us?

CAN I ASK YOU A QUESTION?

By Christopher R. Watkins

The recreational league championship brought a trophy for the Jets.
That's where I learned that the thrill of victory is as good as life gets!
I remember Momma in the crowd that night, a
light mist gleaming off her dark hair.
But you were nowhere in sight because you were never there.
A middle school championship was a victory for the Hills.
The memories of that last drive still gives me the chills.
Uncle Pop was in the crowd that night, my enthusiasm he shared.
But you were nowhere to be found because you were never there.
My first high school touchdown pass. I predicted it in the huddle.
Three seconds was all I needed for a high school super bowl shuffle.
The entire crowd went wild. There was electricity in the air.
But as I looked up in the stands I noticed that you weren't even there.
I never won a state title but I graduated all the same.
A blue and gold cap and gown, a plaque that bore my name.
Pictures with Pop and Nina. Momma's shades projected a glare.
But you weren't in any of the pictures because you were never there.
I didn't make it through college but gave the state ten years of my life.
I'll still be young when I'm released with a chance to do things right.
My family team has taken some hits. Anaiyah is its newest player.
I feel like I've lost the other side because you were never there.
Momma told me that you played football too. You were good back then.
I missed out on all your tips and advice. I'll
never know what could have been.
But one day, I know I plan to be a father. And I know I plan to be there.
So, can I ask you a question, Dad? Did you ever even care?

THE REAL DEPARTMENT OF CORRECTIONS (IN GEORGIA)

I would like to dedicate this last portion of this publication to the men and women who are still physically confined within the razor wire and walls of the Department of Corrections. This is for those who are physically and mentally subjected to the oppression and assault from those who claim to stand for justice and righteousness. For ten long, grueling years I lived in the same situation I have just described, and I have made it my sworn duty to expose what those whom I have left behind continue to endure.

The book, entitled "The New War", was written at a time in my incarceration when I finally had a major epiphany. It took me nine years to finally come to the realization that even though we were aggravated, irritated, mentally, physically; and, emotionally abused on a daily basis, we were not actually fighting the people who wore the uniforms and badges. Black people believe that there is a cliché in the White community that says, "If you want to hide something from Black man, place it in a book". As a child, I never liked to read, and the only books that I ever found interesting enough to pick them up was a series of novels by R. L. Stine called "Goosebumps". These books were a series of horror stories for kids that were very popular when I was in the fifth grade. Needless to say, I believe that this is where I developed a love for novels of that particular nature. When I became incarcerated, I discovered the books by Dean Koontz.

In addition to reading the novels by Dean Koontz, I also began to crave knowledge. This lead me to pick up a book entitled, "Behold a Pale White Horse", by William Cooper. For me, this book was the confirmation of the power of knowledge. Mr. Cooper begins the book by introducing himself thoroughly. However, just in case anyone is in doubt about his credentials, there are official documents in the back of the book proving that he is who he claims that he is. In the very first chapter, Mr. Cooper goes into detail about a situation where simply knowing too much and speaking out on the information can cause one's life to be threatened which was the case for him. Mr. Cooper was actually killed in November 2001, but questions continue to go unanswered concerning his death. It appears that Mr, Cooper was assassinated because of his knowledge.

The "War' that I referred to is not racial or religious. The war that I am referring to is the one between the ignorant and the knowledgeable. I wanted to mention the Willie Lynch story here, but, I absolutely, with every fiber of my being, do not want this writing to be about race. I believe that the only reason that race is an issue in what I am about to say is because Blacks are in the majority in the prison system[181]. Allow me to take a different approach and paint a picture for you here. Let's begin with the Officer on duty who has been on the same job for almost two decades; and, according to him, "has seen it all". He goes home every day to a wife whom he argues with religiously. The bills are past due; and, the doctor has just told his wife that she has lost the baby they have been so patiently trying and waiting to have. The other children of the family are running wild. His car needs some serious, costly work; and, if that isn't enough, he is running on about three hours of sleep.

Now, let's meet one of the inmates who has been incarcerated longer than the majority of the population around him has been alive. He sleeps in a tiny cell with two younger bunk-mates who have no respect for their elder roommate. They stay up all night and talk extremely loudly about things that have absolutely no relevance to their present situation. They won't clean up behind themselves so the cell is filthy. Just about all of this man's family members, that he was close to anyway, have died so he has no one to send money to him, to visit him; or, to send mail to him. This inmate wakes up every day, goes out to a work detail where he is worked like a dog for a peanut butter and jelly sandwich or a turkey sandwich, only to come back; and, regardless of the temperature, have to strip naked for inspection before returning to his cell. As if this is not enough, his counselor called to tell him to forget about being paroled because the parole board has just decided to put his parole off for another eight years.

One morning, the inmate in question is sent to the laundry to pick up more sheets for his bed because his two roommates accidentally spilled something on his bed during the night. His roommates had never gone to sleep that night, but, had been talking, arguing, eating and drinking all night. Tired and hungry, since he has no one to send him money to buy food that he may have in his room to snack on, this inmate makes his way to the laundry to get clean sheets for his bed. He puts his clothes on; tucks

---

18   1

his shirt into his pants; tightens his belt; and, ties his shoes all the way up to the second hole. He throws all of his other affects into his pocket and rushes to make it out of the door before the officer in the security booth suddenly has a change of heart and tells him he cannot go to the laundry after all. Did I fail to mention that this inmate is being held against his will?

The Officer on duty, that morning in the security booth, had awaken this morning with his wife yelling at him about something he felt was really irrelevant to him. After she runs out of the door because she woke up late and is about to be late to her job; he finds it is his job to wake the kids up and get them fed and ready for school. He scrambles up a breakfast from almost nothing while arguing under his breath about why his wife has not been to the grocery store to buy food. He feeds the children and gets them ready for school. Finally, he's ready to go and his car won't start! He had left the lights on all night and now needs a jump start to get the car going. He makes his way to his neighbor's house aggravated, irritated and tired from lack of sufficient sleep. When he finally arrives at work, he is assigned to the area he dislikes the most, the walk outside the 'chow hall' or inside the 'chow hall'.

Now the inmate has stood at the laundry for thirty minutes waiting to receive the clean sheets for his bed. When the lady in charge of the laundry finally comes out to help him, she informs him that the Deputy Warden of Care and Treatment has issued a decree that without a clothing request, he can't have anything from the laundry. Feeling his burdens bearing down on him, he returns to his dorm room. Everyone is now on their way to breakfast, but the dorm officer suddenly has amnesia and forgets where the inmate has been all of this time. Now, the inmate has to get the lady in charge of the laundry to verify that he has been there because without her word, he will not be allowed to have breakfast. He goes back to the laundry, stands there again waiting for the lady to sign his form. After ten more minutes, the inmate is finally ready for breakfast. Now finally he can go eat.

Having received the necessary clearance, the inmate is calmly on his way to eat. He walks down the hall the right way to the cafeteria. He has shaved himself this morning before going out. He makes sure his shoes are all tied and his belt is tight on his waist so that his pants don't fall. After all of his preparation and aggravation this morning, as soon as he walks into the Chow Hall, he is greeted by the one person that may have had the worst morning of his life, the Officer on duty. Tired and aggravated, not in the mood but posted in the Chow Hall to monitor the behavior of the inmates as they enter and leave; the Officer is obediently on his most hated posted. His temper is short. His coffee mug is empty, and, in his mind, he seems to have more than enough reasons to possess a vindictive attitude. In walks the inmate, and the one thing he has forgotten, the Officer immediately sees. "Hey you! Yeah, I'm talking to you! Bring your #%* over here." says the Officer to the inmate. Being the man he is diligently trying to become, the inmate calmly shakes his head, laughs it off, and, reports to the Officer. "Where is your I.D?" the Officer inquires. The inmate honestly didn't realize that he was missing his I.D. "Sir, I forgot it, Sir." Jack replies. "Go get it!" The Officer demands. Now the inmate has to go all the way back around to his building to get an item that is really unnecessary, since the Officer already knows him well. But the inmate not only wants to eat, but, he needs to eat. However, the Officer radios the building to tell them, not that the inmate is coming, but, to not allow him to leave the building. The Officer tells the officer in Jack's building, "Do not let his %&* back out the door."

Unaware of the conversation that has transpired, the inmate grabs his I.D. and starts back out of the building only to be informed by the person in the booth that the Officer in Charge (O.I.C.) has instructed them to keep him in the building and not allow him out. This was the proverbial 'straw that broke the camel's back'. The inmate becomes enraged.

I can recall that when I was assigned to the State Prison from 2006 to 2008, I had a similar situation one morning and was unjustly denied a meal. That morning I was the last inmate to leave the building for breakfast. When I arrived at the door of the Hall, it appeared that the officer on duty locked eyes with me right before the door slammed in my face. There were three of us and we began to beat on the door and window of the booth because we wanted to go in to eat. When the door finally opened, we found ourselves face to face with a higher ranking officer who, of course, appeared to agree with his subordinates on duty. This was a common occurrence that I had witnessed, even if the subordinates were wrong in their actions. The officers confronted us as long as we would stand there and argue, but, they would not allow us to go in and eat. We never heard an explanation as to why we could not go in and eat. These kinds of things occur over and over again, every day in the center.

In the first situation with the inmate and the Officer in charge, I don't believe that the I.D. was the issue. I believe that the real issue was the fact that Officer had a badge and authority and the inmate did not. Why couldn't the Officer in charge have told inmate not to come back in the first place? Why would he have told the inmate to go back and get his I.D., then call the officer in the booth and tell them something totally different? I have witnessed countless individuals appear to become victims of this type of abuse in G.D.C. system every day. I don't believe that the problem was the fact that the inmate didn't have his I.D. After all of the examples of abuse that I have witnessed and also been the victim of during my ten years in the G.D.C., I believe that the problem was exactly as I stated above – the fact that the Officer had a badge of authority and the inmate did not, and, he was an inmate in a prison system. It appeared to me that because of the situations that landed us in the prison system and caused us to bear the title 'inmate', regardless of the circumstances surrounding that situation, we were now 'third-class' citizens, not as good as those who were hired to watch over us.

I recall that while I was at Prison in GA, one of the officers, was placed under investigation for orders that he had issued to one of the Conflict Emergency Response Team (CERT) teams to beat an inmate. The young man was then placed in what was called the 'hole', a place of solitary confinement. Those of us who shared the same building with this young man knew that he had not been involved in a physical altercation. However, the autopsy performed on this young man revealed physical bruises all over his body. This was not the first or last time that this sort of thing happened. Every time this happened, the Captain and his accomplices, the officers on the CERT, would be absent from work the next few days. What were they running from?

In my experienced opinion, the D.O.C. Is not about rehabilitating and helping an individual to become a productive citizen in society. On the contrary, from my experience in the G.D.C., it is a multi -million dollar industry with people as its main product. Georgia is the only state that does not pay its offenders for services rendered. I could not believe that this is legal in the state of Georgia. It appeared that in 2005 slavery was still supported by the Constitution of the United States of America! The 13th Amendment, section one states as follows: "Neither slavery not involuntary servitude, 'except as punishment for a crime, whereof the party shall have been duly convicted', shall exist in the United States or any place subject to its jurisdiction." This says to me that 'slavery and involuntary servitude are legal in the prison system'! Perhaps this is why so many of the officers would point out to us, the inmates, that we had no rights in the system. I believe that a human being ought to have some rights in any and all situations of life. How is this helping anyone to become a productive citizen to lock them away in slavery and involuntary servitude for whatever number of years? I believe that the police and the prison system form the largest legal, organized "GANG" in America. And, they are equipped to kill at a moment's notice!

From what I could determine from my research and experience, the grievance process is also flawed. Every grievance, whether right or wrong, must go through a process where they may be rejected for any reason, at any time. For example, with a female Deputy Warden, at a State Prison in South Georgia, I don't believe that any grievance ever actually left the institution. This Deputy Warden was, in my opinion, cocky enough to tell us that she was not worried about any grievance because she was confident that her boss would always rule in her favor. She was not the only one to constantly inform the inmates that they were not concerned about any grievances. They would inform the inmates that we could call or write whoever we desired, nothing would change!

When I was assigned to a State Prison in South Georgia; from 2008 – 2014; I was able to spend approximately three of those years in what was labeled the 'Faith and Character' based program. I believed that this was another attempt to better myself, however, it appeared that the officers of the institution ***"HATED THE INMATES OF THE FAITH AND CHARACTER BASED PROGRAM"!!!*** It seemed that there was always an attempt to hinder any progress that we were trying to make! Every year, a class of about twenty inmates were graduated from the program in a special ceremony for the inmates and their family members. The Deputy Warden of Security would only give $200 to spend towards a ceremony and lunch for all of the inmates involved and their family members who attended. The Chaplain would raise approximately $2,000 without the help of the institution, probably from family members and outside ministries. As the Chaplain explained, he would purchase all of the food and tell the officers that the food was only for the inmates and their families. However, on this particular occasion, officers were angered and revenge was planned.

According to the Chaplain, when the very next graduation was planned, he did the same thing as before. He raised the same amount of money, purchased the food, etc. The Chaplain was sent to handle another assignment so that he was away from the food when it was delivered. The officers and other employees on duty stole so much food from the intended lunch that some family members could only receive extremely small portions from food that many of them had contributed to provide. According to the Chaplain, he returned from the other assignment to find a catastrophe. I was there also to witness this situation. I thought that 'theft by taking' was a crime. Of course, nothing was done because, as other employees explained, no one actually saw anyone take the food items from the delivery.

I believe that there will always be a huge population of inmates in the Georgia State Prison System or Georgia Department of Corrections because it has become a mulit-million dollar industry where the inmates are the product or source of the income. Several years ago, inmates could receive packages from home with cosmetics and basic toiletries. Now, everything an inmate receives must come from a catalog where the prices exceed store value. Disciplinary reports (D.R.'s) are written for anything and everything. Whether valid or not, a guilty conviction is given because with a guilty conviction an inmate can be charged $4.00. Imagine receiving $4.00 each day from 1,600 individuals. When an individual becomes ill or needs to be seen by the medical staff, there must be at least $5.00 to $10.00 in that individual's account, or, he will not be allowed to even be seen by a member of the medical staff. I believe that all of these things happen because there are so many individuals incarcerated whose family members are not present and no one else is there to be that advocate in their lives.

I don't believe that these items I have mentioned are a problem just in the state of Georgia. Law enforcement problems are happening all over the country at different levels. It begins with cases like Michael Brown or

Trayvon Martin; or, the Troy Davis execution. I believe that these incidents happen partly because we are governed and ruled by a system that, in 2015, continues to be biased against Blacks, Hispanics and what they consider to be lower class Whites. For example, after my co-defendants and I were convicted of armed robbery, a couple of white girls committed the exact same crime in the same area of the state. While the three of us were given a mandatory ten years in prison, these girls were labeled "the Barbie Bandits", laughed at and slapped on the wrist with probation. It seems to me that every level of the system operates on stereotypes and bias.

One doesn't have to be a rocket scientist to understand what is happening in the department of corrections. I believe that individuals in the system are aware of and understand the things they are doing wrong. I also believe that when they know that there are individuals on the outside that will speak up and do something about what is happening, they are a bit more hesitant concerning the things they do. I believe that it is time for us to do something about reforming the system. Just because an individual commits a crime does not cause that person to no longer be a human being. The kind of injustices that I have outlined here are the kinds of things that happen, I believe, when a system is left to regulate and police itself. The grievance process is simply telling the system about the system. The last time that I checked, the Declaration of Independence read, "We hold these truths to be self-evident, that all men are created equal..." As long as I am still a man, a living, breathing human being, I am entitled to be treated as equal to every other human being. It appears that the Corrections System doesn't think so. This is a problem that deserves our best effort.

A NEW WAR

There is a New War in progress, a new battlefield taking shape,
A new enemy on the horizon, with new weapons, a new face.
The future looks so dim and dreary, lives
will be lost at a devastating place.
Children will grow up parent-less, In this lawless, chaotic place.
These new, calculated attacks have quickly
and critically crippled our troops.
The fear of black and white leaves soldiers shaking in their boots.
Where is our ally in these trying time? How can we combat the masses?
Where do we find the friend we need to burn these fiends to ashes?
Traditional tactics no longer are effective.
Physical fighting will not work.
Only the knowledge of Noble men can defend
our future from what lurks.

By Christopher Randolph Watkins

Printed in the United States
By Bookmasters